A COUNTRY WAR

Memoirs of a Land Girl

Best Wishes
Enjoy the book
'Micky Mitchell'
(Maud Shine)
5:01:08

A COUNTRY WAR
Memoirs of a Land Girl

Micky Mitchell

HALSGROVE

First published in Great Britain by Halsgrove, 2007

British Library Cataloguing-in-Publication Data
A CIP record for this title is available from the British Library

ISBN 978 1 84114 650 8

HALSGROVE
Halsgrove House
Ryelands Farm Industrial Estate, Bagley Green,
Wellington, Somerset TA21 9PZ
T: 01823 653777
F: 01823 665294
email: sales@halsgrove.com
website: www.halsgrove.com

*The front cover photograph shows the author in her Land Army uniform,
aged seventeen. The back cover shows the badge of the Women's Land Army
from an embroidered version made by the author.*

Printed in Great Britain by Cromwell Press, Trowbridge

Foreword

The purpose of these memoirs is to enlighten my children, grandchildren and hopefully generations to come, about the conditions under which we existed during World War II. In particular it depicts the years I spent in the Women's Land Army and hopefully it contains an element of history too. I never kept a diary – life was too busy – so the title of these chronicles is apt. They are plain and simply a record of my memories, one event leading on to the next, incident following incident. I tell it how it was. I have been amazed at how vividly I recall these times. I have relived them with every stroke of the pen, on occasions actually laughing out loudly at the amusing occurrences.

Yes, I have shed some tears too. But that is life. The girls who volunteered for this form of service to their country worked so very hard, putting in long hours for a pittance. One ex-Land girl who was recently invited to a reunion at Totnes said, "It was out and out slave labour, instigated by men for the benefit of men". Yet though the work was extremely hard and the hours long, it certainly had its compensations in friendships that were forged and the humour that prevailed in dangerous times. Most of the girls forfeited secure, well paid jobs and comfortable homes for a primitive life style but few shirked these conditions or even objected. We were very young. I was just seventeen years old when I started my training having forsaken a position of Post Office Counter Clerk, a job with excellent prospects. Now we are old but the wonderful memories will always remain.

So read on, my children, and know that I too was once young.

Maud Shire
Honiton
2007

The author in her Land Army uniform, aged seventeen.

DEDICATION
FOR MY BELOVED FAMILY

Alan, my husband

∾

Margaret, Rosemary, Elaine, Vanessa and Alan, our children

∾

Mandy, Michelle, Sharon, Martyn, Mark, Shawn, Adrian, Shelley, Kade, Kyra, Jake, Alex, Luke and Josh, our grandchildren

∾

Eric, Lindsay, Zak, Brittany, Devon, Amber, Emma, Alysia, Daniel, Oliver, Sophie, Jessica and Katie, our great grandchildren

Contents

Maud Shire c.1954

The Long, Long Journey

I was barely seventeen years old and here I stood on this smoky, smelly platform at Blackburn railway station.

Nowadays stream trains are romanticised with a following of fanatics who dedicate every spare minute and much hard cash for their preservation. The engines are cleaned and polished with love and adoration. 'Steam' fanatics tend them carefully, worshipping every shining brass plate and gleaming painted surface but my early memories of them bring to mind grimy, noisy, unwashed, mighty giants belching steam and polluting the atmosphere with smoke and fumes. But then I am a woman and I have never really appreciated the finer science of engineering in any way shape or form. A working steam train, in my youth, was by no means such a glamorous object.

It was with some trepidation that I waited. My family had come to see me off on what was so far the greatest and most exciting adventure of my young life. You see today was the culmination of weeks of interviews and examinations which lead to my being accepted as a member of The Women's Land Army and I had been posted to a training farm in Devon prior to placement on a dairy farm in the West Country. I was going to the mixed farm at Whimple owned by Mr Robert Whiteway (of cider fame) and as I had scarcely put a foot outside of Lancashire, to me it was like being posted to the other side of the world.

A look of pride flitted across my mother's face as she looked at me and I must admit that I felt very smart in my riding breeches and jacket, my brimmed felt hat at a jaunty angle, knee high stockings pulled up over the laced leg of the breeches and brown brogues, shining brightly (the result of daily polishing from the very first day I had acquired them). The only splash of colour came from the green pullover and armband which I wore and, of course, the Women's Land Army badge which I proudly sported on the band around my hat. Under my sweater I wore a dark cream coloured cotton shirt with the Land Army tie and this ensemble was my 'dress' uniform. All my other possessions along with my working clothes were neatly packed into a battered, old, second-hand suitcase mother had managed to find for me. It was very shabby but then this was wartime and I was lucky to possess a suitcase at all.

As I stood there I was fervently wishing that my train which was overdue would pull into the station. I dreaded the motion of saying my 'Goodbyes' to all the people I loved so much and I recall the relief I felt when it eventually pulled in alongside the platform. I looked up at the filthy, blackened glass roof whilst the smoke from the train swirled upwards and the steam hissed and rose to intermingle with the other polluting emissions. There were forms at intervals along the platform but nobody used them for fear of getting sooty smudges on their clothes and I most certainly wasn't prepared to soil my lovely new uniform.

With a hoot and a hiss the train slowed down and came to a halt and there was a hustle and bustle as carriage doors were flung open and an endless stream of people alighted, all making a dash for the station steps leading to the underpassage then up to the station exit. The time had come at last for me to board the train. My Uncle Jim took charge of my suitcase. He carried it onto the train placing it above the seats on a net rack. Then he reserved a seat for me whilst I hugged and kissed each member of my family and said my 'Goodbyes'. Tears trickled down my mother's cheeks and I bit my lip in an attempt to be brave as I assured her that the time would soon pass and I would be home on leave. Eventually the porter passed along the platform slamming the carriage doors. Uncle Jim jumped down and with a passing farewell I took my seat. After a whistle and a shunt or two the train slowly moved forward... at last I was on my way. Excitement bubbled up inside me... my great adventure had really begun!

It seemed that no sooner had the train started, passed over a few bridges (giving frightening views – eye-level views of filthy black buildings, one on top of another) than the train stopped – we were at Darwen Station. Immediately came to mind that other time, just a few years past when I had my first encounter with Darwen and once again I was the lost and lonely child – lost because at just twelve years of age I had been plucked away from my family to be evacuated. I was a World War II evacuee and it was a terrifying ordeal.

One day my mother, older sister Molly and younger sisters May and Margaret were together at our new home in Harpurley, Manchester, trying to weave back the broken threads of family life after a disturbing and traumatic breakdown of our mother's and father's marriage when suddenly we were at war with Germany. I set out for school on that September day not knowing if or when I would ever return home again feeling deep down inside that I would never, ever meet up with my family again. You see I was to be evacuated with Harpurley High School for Girls, the school I elected to attend on passing my scholarship, whereas my mother together with my baby nephew, Barrie, and my two young sisters were to be "shipped off" with Alfred Street School, to goodness knew where! As far as I was aware we could be sent to opposite ends of the universe and for many months I truly believed this was what had happened. Those months of uncertainty and sheer aloneness still fill me with dread.

Having been herded on to our coaches, identity tags (ie. baggage labels) attached to coat lapels and boxed gas masks slung over our shoulders and across our chests, we set out into the great unknown.

Our first stop was at the Victoria Railway Station, Manchester, and here our bewildered group were ushered on to a train.

I had not been attending my school for long. At that point I had not had chance to socialise with my classmates – oh, I got on well with all the girls but did not have one particular mate unless one could count Georgina who had shared my desk at school but then Georgina had an older sister, Christina, attending the same school and who, of course, had taken her young sister under her wing.

And so it had been a tired, frightened and lonely little girl who had stepped down on to the platform at Darwen Station, this very same station at which we had stopped.

As we alighted from our carriages our teachers told us to walk in pairs so that a long snake of children slithered its way from the station to the market square and thence to a large Victorian School. Here it was bedlam! Nobody seemed to know what was happening – some children sat around sobbing. Others free from parental control chased around nilly-willy. Georgina had wet her knickers and I was trying to get her to a toilet when Christina came over and took charge.

Suddenly amidst the chaos a lady appeared on a platform and rang a bell. All went silent and she told us we were to be given an iced bun and a glass of lemonade. Cheers rang out – we were all ravenous – and we all started to queue for our refreshment.

After a while a system emerged whereby a teacher would call out the name of a child who would then step up to a table where they were furnished with a name and an address of the family with whom they would be staying. Sadly I waved to Georgina and her sister as they left together, taxied away by the many volunteers who were fortunate enough to own cars. When my turn came I was given the name of a young lady whose husband was a sailor and I was just about to set out for her home at Sunnyhurst when a man dashed up to the car and said I must return to the school hall as the person with whom I was to have been billeted had been rushed to hospital.

It was dark outside and the hall was almost empty when I was finally taken to stay with a middle-aged widow and her son, Ivor, who at a guess I'd say was around thirty years old. Ivor was extremely kind to me. However, his mother who had not wished to take in an evacuee in the first place was a different kettle of fish .... But that's another story and in the past.

Now I must look to the future – my future in Devon. A new start, a new life whatever that would entail. I just need to show you that as a result of these experiences so early in my life, I was quite independent and self-sufficient having fended for myself from a very early age.

As the train slowed down and came to a halt followed by the hustle and bustle of luggage being taken down from overhead racks and passengers exiting and boarding, I glanced across the railway lines to the opposite platform. The billboards were just as they had been five years ago. The slogan "Be like Dad – Keep Mum" was from its scratched and mutilated condition probably the original one. Then the train resumed its journey, under the familiar bridge, which spanned Marsh House Lane. I was suddenly overcome by the nostalgia of my years spent in this town. The memories are good ones overall.   It was here I experienced my first 'boy and girl' courtship with Bobby, my first romantic kiss. Above all I owed so much to the Staff at Darwen Grammar School who encouraged me academically and supported me in my physical efforts on the sports field. To this day I vow that no school could have helped to shape my future as did my tutors and, yes, my peers at this seat of learning.

As we slowly passed under the bridge the hissing and the screeching whistle signalled a faster pace culminating with the "diddle-de-dum, diddle-de-dee" of wheels on track as we approached the moors beyond.

I felt a tug at my heartstrings and said a silent farewell to the many friends who had played such a vital part in my growing up. "Goodbye, Darwen" you'll always hold a place in my heart.

The old steam train trundled onwards, dropping off and taking on its human cargo and we were soon steaming in to the Station in the city of Manchester. Taking my battered old suitcase from the overhead rack and slinging my travel bag over my shoulder I jumped down to the platform ready to tackle the next stage of my journey on my great adventure. Knowing the city as I did I realised it would be a tiring trek across to London Road Station beladened with my luggage. For a while I toyed with the idea of hailing a taxicab but decided to save what little cash I had by putting my best foot forward. I was young and strong and completely fascinated by the motley of humanity I encountered. Service men and women from the armies, navy's and airforces of many nations world-wide mingling with civilians busily going about their business – it was certainly not the city I remembered from my childhood. Because of my interest and curiosity at the passing world, the task of getting from station to station was easier than I had anticipated and I was soon striding up the street that formed a broad ramp to the station's entrance.

By this time I was feeling hungry and thirsty so I made my way to the refreshment car. As on numerous other occasions during my time in the Women's Land Army, I was instantly offered a seat by a well-mannered airman (well those breeches and the slouched brim of the hat did do something for a girl, didn't they?) However, I insisted on paying for my own half pint of shandy and stayed there conversing with one person and then another until it was time to board my train. Again I was very fortunate in securing a comfortable seat by the window, probably because I was there so early. By the time the train was due to leave it was "bursting at the seams", every seat was occupied and people were packed like sardines in every nook and cranny of corridor space. The passengers were mainly composed of service men and women but I did not see another Land Girl amongst them.

Checking that my train pass and purse were in a safe place I settled down in my snug little corner. The station stops were limited on the journey – I recall short sojourns at Stockport and Crewe but after this the train picked up speed as it hurtled through the night on the long, long journey to Penzance. The time of departure from Manchester had been midnight and after the long, exciting but tiring day I fell asleep. The jerks of the train as it pulled out of Shrewsbury and then Hereford temporarily disturbed my sleep but hazily I was soon back to sleep lulled by the rocking and swaying of the carriage. At Bristol I stirred and fought and scrambled my way to the toilets returning to my seat refreshed and wide-awake and ready for the packed meal, which my dear mum had insisted, I take with me.

On leaving Bristol the landscape viewed through the window changed markedly. Gone were the dry stone walls peculiar to the North and in their place were green, hand-built hedges filled with wild flowers and foliage and topped by sprouting young trees and shrubs. Some had been newly laid and were very neat – the two methods of sectioning off fields, one northern and one southern, were completely different. Noticeably too was the red earth of a fallow field, the vivid green of the grass and young crops and the clean, sparkling appearance of the countryside in general. After all there were no cotton mills here bellowing out black, sooty smoke from their tall chimneys. I was completely enchanted by this "new land", the beautiful fields like a patchwork quilt woven by Mother Nature herself – one patch of red earth, one gold (the stubble of newly harvested corn) one dark green (ready to harvest potatoes) and another pale green (young growth of Winter greens). Now we were in Somerset and the terrain was flat and the low-lying fields were separated by water dykes. These are known as the Somerset Levels and this area produced willow for basket weaving.

The train gradually slowed down and came to a halt at Taunton Station so that I realised I was nearing my destination, Exeter in Devon. I took out my notebook in order to study and plan the remaining route for my journey to Whimple and Mr Whiteway's training farm where I was to spend the next four weeks. During these last few miles I had managed to describe, in rhyme, my observations and feelings in my notebook. This was a habit I had acquired as it came easily to me. Unfortunately I never kept copies but after I had settled in at Whimple I sent them all to my mother. She was very impressed and proudly passed them around for family members and friends to read and even today I receive complimentary remarks from those who had read my 'poetry'.

Jumping down onto the platform at St David's Station in Exeter to the wolf whistles and calls from sailors who were presumably resuming their journey to their Naval base at Plymouth, I checked my travel pass, put my purse in a safe, convenient place, picked up my suitcase and set off in the direction of the station exit. I had been very economical with the small amount of cash at my disposal so far and I decided to take a taxi cab to Exeter Central Station, firstly because I had no idea how to get there but mainly because I could see that the directions given to me by a porter meant climbing a steep hill (St David's Hill). However, as it turned out the distance was short. Up the hill the cab took me, around a clock tower and about two hundred yards further along the route we arrived at the station's entrance. The cab driver very kindly advised me that there was an excellent facility for men and women of any nationality just a few minutes walk along the street. My priority now was to check out the time my next train connection was due – this would be the final leg of my long, long journey. I paid and tipped the cab driver thanking him for his advise and went in to ascertain the time my train would leave for Whimple. I how had a two-hour wait in Exeter and decided to stroll down Queen Street and check out this wonderful canteen of which the cab driver had been so complimentary.

What a blessing this establishment proved to be! "The Allied Services Club", which is now the Exeter Museum was run by the WVS. All members of the forces received a warm welcome during these war years, in addition to freshly made sandwiches and scrumptious home-made cakes and scones. I now entered for the first time and having purchased a scone and a mug of tea, seated myself at one of the many tables, I took stock of my surroundings. The huge room with high ceilings had a wonderful atmosphere. It was full of service people. Because of the invasion and landings of the Allied troops in France this part of the country had a concentration of soldiers, sailors and airmen of every conceivable race. I noticed a group of Australian Anzacs identifiable by the large brimmed, felt hat (the brim was held in place from back to front on one side by their regimental badge). There were exiled Polish Airmen, Free French Forces, many, many US servicemen and last, but not least, a smattering of our own "boys".

Even though it was midday most of the many tables were occupied presumably with clientele like myself, whiling away the time between trains prior to reporting for duty or starting leave. I cannot recall ever seeing a coloured person there. At this period in history coloured people in the US services were segregated from the white – of course, they were welcome to lay down their lives for their country but not to mix with their white American compatriots! I know from later discussions on the subject with Yanks that they found it difficult coming to terms with the fact that our attitude was different – we actually spoke to coloured people and treated them as equals!!! Of course, then as now, there were racists amongst us but our priorities were freeing the peoples of Europe who were under the Nazi heel and it was, for us, a concerted effort. Perhaps World War II was the turning point, albeit only a beginning, in the emancipation of the American coloured population which eventually, after many future years of struggle, brought them equality of human rights.

Time passed by quickly and I realised that I must resume my journey so retracing my steps I soon found myself on platform three in Central Station. The train was prompt and in no time at all I was aboard and travelling at a slow pace. After the Badgers' Holt stop the speed increased .... To Pinhoe then Broadclyst, names of villages that to me were magical. On leaving Broadclyst I noticed acre upon acre of apple orchards, precisely planted rows of trees, equidistant from each other and all heavily laden with fruit. On higher orchard slopes stood a row of gigantic white letters W.H.I.T.E.W.A.Y.S each letter towering high above the trees and it was then that I realised my long, long journey was ending – this for the next month was to be my base where I would train as a dairymaid. Of course, Mr Whiteway and his family were world renowned for the production of cider and it was here in the village of Whimple where the apples were harvested, transported to the cider factory and the end product was delicious. In addition to these fruits grown locally in his own backyard, he purchased apples from fruit growers and farmers around the area and it was a certain type of apple that made the best cider.

At last the train stopped and as I stepped down I began to feel the effects of my journey and this weariness, combined with more than a little apprehension about my future, made me feel very tired indeed. I slowly ambled along the lane in my quest to find the Land Army Hostel. It was a beautiful little village and very quiet. There was no sign of a Land Girl as I passed the Square and Village Shop/Post Office.

"I 'spose thees looking for thic there Land Army Hostel?" The voice belonged to a middle aged man and he quickened his pace until he was walking alongside me.

"I am," I replied, "Could you direct me please?"

"Well, maid, I'es off to the Fountain, landlord wants a hand. Gie me your case and I'll tek yer," he retorted and with the same he grasped my luggage and strode forward.

It was only a very short distance to the pub, The New Fountain Inn, but he proceeded past its entrance and continued up the lane. Suddenly, he stopped, put my case down and instructed me on where to go next.

*The New Fountain
Inn, Whimple.
Little changed since
the author's first
visit.*

Actually I was virtually there at the gates of the hostel.

"Thank you so much," I said.

"Right" was all he said as he turned and retraced his steps back to the Inn.

Arrival

I was here at last. There was a semi-circular stone built wall with a central gate entrance with a pathway weaving up to the front door of this beautiful old house. For a short while I leaned against the stone wall and took in the peace and beauty of this lovely building before strolling up the path to the front door where I rang the bell and was admitted.

A lady supervisor greeted me and after a brief interview, she asked a young girl to show me around. The kitchen was out of bounds to all except the kitchen staff. It was situated at the rear of the building and alongside was the dining room, a large room with trestle-type tables running lengthways down the room – basic but adequate. Either side of each table were forms.

Downstairs was a quiet lounge with easy chairs, occasional tables, bookshelves and a large open fireplace. Then there was a recreation room with a small stage at one-end and table tennis facilities. I recall that every two weeks, ENSA put on a show for us. It was on Wednesday and on this night we were not allowed out – we were all expected to support these "artistes". From the hall we climbed the stairs to the first floor. (Beyond this floor I never ventured except when, on one occasion when a Land Girl friend partook of too much cider down at the New Fountain. Several of us physically had to carry her back and, amidst struggle and giggles, we endeavoured to secrete her up two flights of stairs and put her to bed without disturbing supervisor. What a laugh that was!). I was then shown the toilet and bathroom before entering a huge bedroom. This bedroom faced the front of the house and from the large window overlooked a somewhat overgrown garden. I liked this room immediately despite the fact that the furnishings etc were somewhat austere. There were three sets of bunk beds and as I was the first of my group to arrive I was invited to choose which bed I wanted. I selected the top bunk of the beds nearest the large window. I was then shown where to put my belongings (a wardrobe and two chests of drawers to be shared between the six of us).

"Dinner will be each evening at 6," my chaperone declared and exited.

The view of the garden was relaxing – just shrubs, trees and a somewhat neglected lawn and something I had never seen before, huge clumps of pampas grass. I studied the wardrobe and decided that there should be

Whimple House, as it looked during the war.

enough space for all our clothes. My own were sparse but then clothing was rationed and we had to hand over our clothing coupons for any textiles. It did not take long for me to hang my civilian clothes in the wardrobe and neatly place underwear and uniform in my allotted drawer. I recall that on the Saturday all six girls in the dormitory agreed to share each other's clothes. We were all fairly average size-wise although I was 38-26-36 which meant I had problems in some instances trying to fasten blouse buttons and another girl, Marjorie, was shorter than the rest of us but on the whole it was fun trying on different clothes. We all, of course, kept to our own dress uniform, which was worn with pride, when we went to town.

In retrospect my four weeks at Whimple was one of the happiest periods of my life. The camaraderie between us was wonderful – we were there for each other without any malice – just great fondness.

There was a rota system for training. On our arrival six Land Girls who had trained there for four weeks and having been selected for a certain branch in agriculture, eg. Forestry, Gang, Dairy, were despatched to their various permanent situations. There were already six land girls (in the second floor bedroom) who had been training there for two weeks and so they were expected to 'show us the ropes' before leaving, after a further two weeks, when we would become the seniors and take care of the next six recruits. This system meant that there were always twelve girls on the course at any one time and that we each had four weeks training. Initially we were all trained as Dairy Maids and although the majority of girls passed out as such at the end of the month, just a few would be deemed unsuitable for this kind of farming. They would then be diverted to other types of agricultural work – the very occasional one would be rejected completely.

The farm here at Whimple, was, as I said previously, owned by Mr Whiteway. It was a mixed farm, and in addition to managing a dairy herd, we were expected to be involved with the breeding and rearing of other farm animals, ie. pigs, horses, sheep, etc. Also fieldwork was a very important part of our training. We would eventually end up on small mixed farms so this was sensible. Fieldwork, of course, varied from season to season and, haymaking and harvesting over, it was time to dig and pick up potatoes and collect all those apples for cider-making. There were acre upon acre of orchards growing the special cider apples and the time was ripe for their harvest after which they were taken to the cider factory close to the railway station.

I very quickly unpacked my suitcase and was suddenly overwhelmed by the fatigue brought about by twenty-four hours of non-stop travelling. It was a strange kind of tiredness, not wearying, more like a great wave of relief sweeping over me. I suppose that leaving home at just seventeen years of age, the long journey and the uncertainty of what lay ahead had finally caught up with me, all of a sudden, and now I had arrived and I knew that my immediate future, for at least the next month, would be here. I felt completely relaxed and content. Seated on a chair by the huge window, I gazed over the large unkempt garden. The huge clumps of tall Pampas Grass fascinated me. Other shrubs abounded, all gangly from the need of pruning and I closed my eyes and tried to imagine how this garden must have looked in days gone by, a well-loved haven of peace and tranquillity. Amongst the shrubs and trees perennials struggled for survival and, sadly, many were fighting a losing battle. My eyelids were beginning to droop so I swung myself up to my bunk and in no time at all fell into a deep sleep.

I was abruptly awakened by a hand ruffling my hair.

"Hi there! I'm Alma. Thought I had better give you a shake – it's half past five – I guess you won't want to miss dinner?"

"Hello Alma," I retorted and gazed into a lovely face with large brown eyes, long dark lashes framed by thick, black hair.

"I'm Maud – Maud Mitchell." I slid down to floor level and proffered a hand.

"Maud! Maud! Oh God no! From here on in you shall be Mitch."

She ignored my outstretched hand, put her arms around me and gave me a reassuring hug.

From that day forward Alma and I were pals. For the next four weeks we were inseparable. We must have made a striking contrast, Alma with her beautiful dark looks and her tall, slender, almost boyish figure and me with my fair curly (permed) hair, styled in the "bubble Cut" fashion of the day and my distinctly hour-glass figure.

We quickly splashed water from a basin over our faces and washed our hands before descending to the dining room.

On entering I was amazed to see so many Land Girls altogether. There were twelve Dairy Maids to-be; six halfway through their training and six newly arrived. In addition there was a large gang of girls who were permanently resident there. Each morning they were collected by a truck and taken to farms thereabout and dropped off in groups according to the requisites of the local farmers. They did field work ie. (currently) apple picking, potato and root vegetable harvesting, hedging and ditching, haymaking and harvesting, planting and hoeing – all according to the season. When engaging in conversation with them later, I discovered that most of these girls had an aversion to livestock. In some circumstances it was a fear, particularly of cows and they also relished the full time company of other girls when at work, whereas, as a Dairy Maid life would be comparatively more isolated.

We were all absolutely amazed at the meal put before us. Now my mother was a wonderful cook, very innovative with the meagre food rations we were allotted during wartime. Meat in particular was in very short supply so there was a limit obviously to what the best cook on earth could do in these circumstances. Yet this meal was terrific – thick slices of roast pork (home reared) with lashings of apple sauce, sage and onion stuffing; crackling, roast potatoes, creamed potatoes, greens, carrots and swede in abundance. All this was followed by cook's home-made apple pie and custard.

What a feast after so many years of making do! Throughout my sojourn at this Hostel, Whimple House, the food remained of a very high standard both in quantity and in quality. Almost everything was home grown and what nowadays would be considered organic.

Six Land Girls forming our group had all arrived and when the meal was over the supervisor who had been seated at the head of our table requested that the new recruits accompany her to the lounge. She briefly instructed us on our working arrangements. We were also advised of the curfew times, which were very reasonable. Exceptions to this rule were made on Friday and Saturday evenings or any occasion when the villagers held their local dances.

"But no matter what time you choose to go to bed, one thing is for certain, you turn up on time for work the following day." She then gave us advice on our ablutions and pointed out that we were allowed one bath each per week with a specified depth of three inches of water.

By this time Mr Sandman was really and truly beckoning us but we all voted to take a stroll down to the village before turning in. Passing the New Fountain Inn it was quite tempting to join in with the revelries which were obviously taking place within but we were all very, very tired after our exhausting day we all decided to return to the Hostel and bed.

Alma and I made our quick introductions to our room mates. They were, however, brief, just a matter of names for we were soon in bed and I was asleep as soon as my head hit the pillow.

I was startled into consciousness on the following morning by a sharp rat-tat-tat-tat on the door. We all jumped out of bed simultaneously, taking turns for use of the bathroom and donning our Aertex shirts, dungarees, stockings, pullovers and boots we were soon downstairs. A quick cup of tea and we were very prompt in the reporting for duty in the farmyard.

A very young herdsman asked for two of us to bring the dairy herd in from the field so Alma and I volunteered. It was a beautiful morning as we trudged up the lane and turned left into a by-lane. The sun had barely succeeded in penetrating a dark blanket of mist and, as it did so, it revealed the most glorious countryside I had ever seen. The silver cobwebs covered in dew stretched in lacy profusion from branch to branch of the hedgerows; the grass was covered with an identical silvery dew and the green of the grass, the blue of the fluffy cloud-dotted sky seemed to have been newly coloured, as if from a paint box. In the distance to our left the ground rose gently. Roughly six hundred yards down this lane the cows came into view and they were obviously more accustomed to the routine than we were because they were already assembled around the gate. The herdsman had already demonstrated how to call the cows .... "Cow up!" or really more like "How up!" Alma and I stood on the lowest bar of the gate and hilariously called to cows. It took us a while to get the right inflection (I'm sure even the cows were laughing at us). They seemed to understand because as we threw the gate open they trundled out, one after another. I went on ahead of the herd in order to turn them right at the lane junction and Alma ambled on behind. They certainly took their time and made no attempt to divert from the route obviously knowing the way better than we did and the only real action occurred when a lower ranking beast had the temerity to try and pass its superior only to be put back in place by a short, sharp tap of the horns. Yes, all the cows had horns .... Horns of all shapes, angles and sizes. These were days before horn cauterisation was carried out whilst they were calves. The only hornless cows then were the polls, which were born hornless.

On turning down the lane which ran alongside the hostel we entered the farmyard and each animal filed into its own stall. If one unintentionally took the wrong place, realisation became aware and she gently backed out swinging into her own stall. We had been warned to be somewhat wary of the horns as we each went alongside each cow securing the chain around its neck. Contentedly they stood enjoying the dairy cake and/or hay, which had been placed in each manger. (The quantity of cake supplied to each cow was measured according to that cows milk yield).

The head cowman advised us where to find combs, stiff bristled brushes, cloths and buckets then taught us how to groom each cow prior to milking it – brushing the ridge of the spine and flanks and combing out the tail then washing and drying the udder.

Next came the difficult part, taking a wooden three-legged stool, sitting on the right hand side of the cow, clasping a pail between my knees and milking it. Firmly stroke the teat between thumb and finger, from the base of the udder downwards, then squeeze with a full hand, milking two teats simultaneously using alternative strokes. It sounds so simple but it takes some time to get the knack. In actual fact a couple of girls never did get the idea of it, simple though it seems. I doubt if they had ever seen a cow before coming from inner cities and they were extremely nervous.

I must say I quickly took it in my stride and within two or three days had become quite a strong hand milker. That's what was needed, strength, strength in one's fingers and hands and it certainly made for aching digits for a week or two. I have to smile as I look back and recall the way we struggled trying to practice our milking skills on an artificial rubber udder, which was attached to a sturdy frame and filled with water. What a laugh!

As and when we were deemed to be proficient enough as milkmaids we were placed on a milking rota for the remainder for the month. Then there was the business of weighing and recording the output of each cow. This was done in an immaculate dairy before the milk was poured into a tank above a cooler, sieved and churned ready for transportation.

After the herd had been turned out to graze, it was time to sluice down the cow sheds and hose the courtyard. A large overhead tank for the conservation of rainwater fed a large water trough but it had to be topped up from the mains when the weather was dry. Then it was time to go in for breakfast. It was Saturday and we were now a complete team of six Land Girls.

The Supervisor summoned us to the lounge and standing before a blackboard and easel, she advised us of notepaper and pencils on the mantelpiece. She invited us to take notes as she spoke to us of what our duties were likely to be when we took up our placements stressing that no two farms were the same and that it was up to us to embrace the system of our individual employers.

She advised us of the various seasonal tasks and we were shown samples of corn – wheat, oats, barley and maize. Then we listed breeds of cattle we were likely to be encountering plus their individual values, eg. Devon Reds – quite reasonable milk producers but excellent for fatting up; Jerseys and

Guernsey's – bony frame but producers of rich, high fat, creamy milk; Ayrshire's – mainly milkers; Herefords – fattening; Friesians – good all round beasts for beef or milk; Shorthorns and Red Polls – mainly beef but fair producers of milk.

Then we were made aware of the necessity of a Women's Land Army. The prime purpose being to ensure that our island nation became as self-sufficient in food production as possible. Our merchant navy took enormous risks from German U-boats and E-boars etc patrolling off our shores. It was vital that our merchant fleet gave priority to the importation of arms etc and every ship was required for that purpose. The more food we were able to produce, the less we had to import. Thus we freed these ships. In addition, for every Land Girl placed in this vital work, a man could be released for the armed forces.

"By the way," she ended, "If anyone's interested there is a dance in the Village Hall tonight at 8 pm. May I also remind you that every alternate Wednesday, ENSA will be here to entertain us and it is essential they have an appreciative audience. They will be here this week." With this we were dismissed.

There was a buzz of excitement in our large bedroom and the time had come for proper introductions. Alma introduced me as "Mitch" (the girls preferred Mick so that's what they chose to call me – Mick, sometimes Micky). I then introduced Alma explaining that her home was in Widnes. In turn we learned each other's names and home towns. There was Ruth, a lovely girl with long, fair wavy hair and she came from Oldham. At the culmination of our period of training she was sent to a farm at Okehampton and I remained in contact with her until she went back home – pregnant. Many, many years later she traced me and spent an afternoon with me an Honiton. Lou – we never knew Lou very well. She was older than the rest of the group. She explained that she was a dramatic actress and had performed on the stage in London. Her home was also in London. She was a very quiet girl, quite introverted, keeping very much to herself. What we considered peculiar was that she carried a flat, silver hip flask with her all the time, wherever she went and surreptitiously took a covert swig from time to time.

We never really knew what the flask contained because after ten days she disclosed that, as she was unsuitable for heavy duty work she was being discharged. She went and we never really knew why. Marjorie was a Jewess and hailed from Liverpool and regrettably we never met again after leaving Whimple. I recall that she confided that her ultimate ambition was to live and work on a Kibbutz in Israel. The sixth girl I just can't recall no matter how much I rack my brain.

After these introductions there was great excitement concerning the village 'hop'. Lou decided to opt out of the dance. "The journey from London

Above: *My Women's Land Army pen pal from Perth, Betty.* Right: *Ruth.*

has wearied me," she said. (So she joined us for a drink at The Fountain, then had an early night.)

So the rest of us were ready for a night on the "town". At barely seventeen years of age, I was the youngest and the others were like big sisters to me. We rested for the remainder of the afternoon and then after dinner it was "action stations". We had pooled our civilian clothes and now we decided to do likewise with our make-up, it was all placed on the chest top giving us more scope when beautifying ourselves. I normally used Ponds Vanishing Cream over which I dabbed a dark shade of loose powder (although I was blond my complexion was quite dark) a dark lipstick and Vaseline on my eyelashes and eyelids; Evening in Paris or Californian Poppy was my choice of perfume.

Alma's contribution to the cosmetic pool was of a more expensive quality than that supplied by the rest of us but she gladly put it out not minding at all. There was chaos in the scramble for the bathroom but we were all eventually washed and dressed, Alma offered to do our make-up. She took such great care with each of us – a job expertly executed. We had decided to wear 'civvies' as it was a dance we were attending and I fancied myself somewhat as we walked down the lane to the Fountain. I clearly remember wearing my royal blue Gor-ray skirt, red and white candy-striped, bishop sleeved blouse and a royal blue sleeveless pullover, which I had knitted myself.

I shall never forget the reaction as we six walked through the door. It was packed to the brim with US servicemen, mainly US sailors with a smattering of flight crews of the USAAF. They crowded around us as if they had never seen a female before. With offers of drinks coming from all direction, we opted to refuse them all and bought our own – three beer shandies and three ciders. It was a wonderful atmosphere – everyone seemed so happy, it was hard to guess there was a war on and these fine young men could soon be going to a possible death. As I stood with four US sailors crowding me out like moths around a flame, I noticed the Landlord beckoning me with a hooked index finger and when I sidled over to the bar he quietly and kindly warned me to watch my drink as it appeared that some of the Yankee sailors had been caught with torpedo juice (TJ), pure alcohol and quite lethal. I duly thanked him and discreetly passed on the information to my mates.

Thirty minutes later we left and made our way to the Village Hall. The locals tried to teach us the Lancers and Quadrille, the Yanks insisted we jitterbug and jive – in return we taught them the Lambeth Walk, The Hokey Cokey and the Palais Glide (they thought these dances were hilarious and soon got the hang of them). We did the Paul Jones when the men walked around the room in Indian File to the music forming an outer circle and the women formed an inner circle moving in the opposite direction. When the music stopped men and women turned to face each other and you danced off with whomsoever your partner proved to be. After so long the marching tune resumed and off you went again in circles. This would be repeated time and time again ensuring the company got to know each other. We danced the slow waltz the quick waltz, the reverse waltz, the quickstep, the slow foxtrot, the Valeta, the Military two-step in addition to the novelty dances and jiving. What great fun it was! Half way through the evening I became aware of a handsome young sailors' attention (mainly because he approached me for nearly every dance). He was very blond, had strikingly blue eyes with a real Adonis physique. He came from Texas, and yes you've guessed, his name was "Tex". I met many more with that nickname within the following month – it seemed that half of Texas was stationed here in Devon!! I also noticed how the Yanks liked nicknames and seldom introduced themselves by their given name – Tex, Spike Al, Joey and so on. However, Tex appeared to be quite nice so I accepted his offer to walk me to the Hostel. I glanced around for my mates and they all appeared to be doing very nicely themselves.

Well, we walked back up the lane to the Big House and I didn't object when he gently slid his arm around my waist. In those times it was, not usual to kiss on a first date but that wasn't the rule for this young jacktar. As we stood by the entrance gate, he suddenly grabbed me with both arms and tried to kiss me and not in a nice way. Then his hands were suddenly everywhere – like an octopus – and I was so scared begging him to let me go. Then we heard laughing and talking as my friends came up the road. The noise and the giggling distracted Tex and as I ran through the gate and up the path I heard him shout, "And NO, I don't want to see you again," quite rudely. I told my "big sisters" of my experience once we were all back inside and they said that they hoped I had learned a lesson. In fact after that night one or another always stuck around unobtrusively whenever we went out socialising.

Apart from our milking rota, we were off duty on the Sunday. A group of us decided to take a stroll through the village and we then turned left along a quiet, winding country lane, eventually realising we were amongst those vast orchards. Pausing, we leaned against a five-barred gate and noticed that although the trees were still laden with fruit the ground beneath was littered with apples, some of which were beginning to rot. Retracing our steps we decided to catch the train into Exeter for the after-noon and evening. At lunch we told cook we would be out for dinner and then set out for Exeter.

Queen Street was heaving with members of the Armed Forces so when we came to a park entrance, we turned left, up a short incline and, through large iron gates. The path led steeply upwards and we soon realised that this was where courting couples held their rendezvous. Exiting near a cas-tle we entered what was once the central shopping area at Exeter – it was now just heap upon heap of rubble. Old Adolf had certainly been up to his tricks here and we were both amazed and relieved when we arrived at the Cathedral to see that it was apparently intact. It is hard to imagine how it was then – no shopping mall or multi-storey car parks. Our detour had brought us back to Queen Street so where else would we go for food but, yes, The Allied Services Club. There was a long queue, but we laughed, joked an did some "people-watching" until the line of customers dimin-ished and we were able to retreat to one certain corner seemingly favoured by the Women's Land Army, and satisfy our appetites.

When we had finished our snack meal we decided to catch the train back to Whimple and have a drink at The Old Fountain for an hour or so before returning for an early night.

Our labours, after all, were about to start in earnest on the following morning.

Descending to the main steps from the Allied Services Club, I felt some one grip my shoulder and turning sharply I peered up into the face of Tex. I shrugged his hand away.

"Come on, baby, I'm sorry. Can't we try again," he said. "I promise to take things at a slower pace." (I took this to mean he was prepared to wait a while this time before jumping on me).

"No way," I retorted emphatically.

Not deterred he tagged on to our group trying to argue his case until we reached the ticket barrier at the station. We girls tramped through in single file.

"Please, Hon!" I heard him shout as I started my way across the bridge.

"Get lost" were my final words to Tex and I guess that's exactly what he did. We never saw him again.

Hands to the Grindstone

Monday morning was the start of our four weeks' of serious training. Our care of the dairy herd was our prime task but, at this time of the year when stock was put out to graze immediately after each milking session, there were approximately five hours of daylight which was utilised before evening milking. During these hours we were familiarised with the other tasks called for one a mixed farm.

In turn and for one day each week we worked in a gigantic shed which housed lots of individual pig pens. Two rows of pens reaching the full length of the shed contained fat pigs; one row held sows in pig and one row sows with suckling piglets. Aisles were placed strategically to facilitate access to feeding troughs, thus enabling us to feed all and sundry without actually entering the pens. The pigman taught us the proportions of swill and pig meal and how to mix it (to a slop) and, of course the quantity of each pen. The swill was the leftover waste food from hotels, restaurants and I guess the abundance of barracks and camps in the area. Outside the entrance to the pig shed was a pig swill sterilizer and apparently this brought the temperature of the waste food up to a degree of heat ensuring complete sterilisation, making the leftovers safe for consumption by the pigs (I believe that this usage of scraps has now been abandoned because the sterilisation process in some cases was incorrectly carried out leaving the swill unsafe for consumption).

In addition we had the task of mucking out the pens – a stinky old job despite the fact that pigs are much maligned in this respect as they keep their house in order by using one specific corner of their abodes as a toilet.

I felt I had an affinity with cows and I really liked the pigs so I felt confident that I was going to enjoy life on the farm when the time came. This farm, as did a few others, used tractors but many more farms, in this part of the country worked the huge Shire horses. Quite frankly, I believe I became something of a "horse whisperer" when my turn to work them came around. Sheep – well I could take them or leave them. To me they always seemed such brainless specimens, timid and uncontrollable except by a couple of sheep dogs and, of course, always using their "follow your leader no matter where" tactics. I was never really keen on the care of poultry either although newly hatched chicks, ducklings and goslings were cute

Lifting potatoes on a Devon farm in wartime using a Fordson tractor.

and, in any case, I later learnt that the farmers wives and daughters usually took on this task.

As I stated previously, apple picking was given priority at this time of the year in this area. Hessian sacks were placed at intervals down through the long, large orchards and each of us laden with a bucket and working in pairs, we picked up all the fallen apples clearing everyone under the first tree before moving on. Up, then down the rows of evenly planted trees we worked, filling our buckets to the brim before emptying them into the sacks placed strategically at intervals in the field. These, in turn, when topped up were collected by a young man with a tractor and trailer and, I presume, hauled back to the cider factory. I made the mistake of picking a luscious looking apple from a tree to eat. One bite and I spat it out. Excellent for cider they may have been but totally inedible, so very bitter and sour.

It wasn't long before we were all groaning about having backache from the many hours of stooping. Let's face it, none of us had done any hard graft; most had worked in offices so this continual bending played havoc with our spines. All the sympathy we got from the regular workers was "You'll get used to it," and we did.

The other back braking job assigned to us was the harvesting of potatoes. Again we would work our way up and down the ranks of potato ridges. The dead foliage of each planted potato pin pointed the spot where we were to dig. I started first with a digger, burrowing as far under the ridge as possible so as not to damage the tubers and Alma followed with a four-pronged pick, sort of raking the turned up soil, ensuring all the potatoes had surfaced. We worked this way until lunch time and then, as the weather was so dry and the potatoes lying on top of the ground had dried off well, we returned to the starting point and picked them up in a similar way to the apples, making sure that any clinging soil was rubbed off using our thumb and fingers. There were acres of spuds to dig and we spent most of our field work time performing this task. Compared to modern systems it all now seems so laborious but few potatoes were damaged or wasted. As the field had been completed, pigs were then allowed to spuddle out any that remained.

One day whilst we were out in the potato field, Alma badly needed to do a wee. She became quite desperate so I went down the field to a young man whose job it was to haul away the sacks, which had been filled. Very embarrassed I explained the situation but he took it all in his stride threw down an empty hessian sack and pointed to the top corner of the field. So off we trouped and I held up the sack as a shield whilst Alma performed and then she stood over and I did my bit – talk about "mod cons".

In all modesty, I had a good strong singing voice and when things began to drag whilst we were doing field work, the gang would shout, "Come on, Mick let's have 'The Last Train to San Fernando' or 'Jealousy'" and I would oblige thus starting a full scale sing-a-long there out in the fields, Alma's favourite was "Brazil ... where hearts were entertained in June, we stood beneath an amber moon and whispered softly some day soon ....." and so on. One of the girls had picked up the naughty lyrics which she put to the tune of 'Jealousy'. I think I remember them.

> *'Twas all over my SOP*
> *It caused all the trouble for me,*
> *For he was an officer in the Raff (RAF)*
> *And I just a poor, little innocent Waff (WAAF),*
> *He gave all his kisses to me*
> *And now I'm a mother to be.*
> *For he was my lover*
> *And now I'm a mother*
> *'Twas all over my SOP.*

(SOP – the abbreviation for Sleeping Out Pass).

We were extremely lucky during our months' sojourn at Whimple – it was early autumn but we had truly wonderful weather. I cannot recall any rain falling for the time we were there – the days were warm and mostly sunny even though it could turn cool in the evenings.

Affaires des Coeurs

At seventeen I had not experienced any in depth relationship, and, as most girls of my age were in these times, I was a virgin. In fact, the only man I ever slept with was the man who I married.

My elder sister had given birth to twins in 1938 whilst single and the shame and unpleasantness almost destroyed our family. In those days sex before marriage was completely taboo and my mother was made a scapegoat simply because she refused to turn my sister out. She not only cared for my sister but she welcomed her home from hospital after the birth of the twins, Barrie and Elaine. Molly was able to bring Barrie home with her but Elaine was a very sick baby and spent all of her young life in hospital succumbing to her illness when she was just three months old. It was all a terrible tragedy but it made me wary for the future when dealing with men. That wasn't ever going to happen to me! That said, I was not immune to the attractions of the opposite sex or vice versa and I was thirteen when I had my first boyfriend. He was called Bobby Ashworth, two years my senior but studying also at Darwen Grammar School. Bobby and I would go to the cinema together, sit on the back row. He would put his arm around me and occasionally kiss me on my lips. He was as shy as I was but we both thought it was so very exciting.

My best friend at school, Doreen, would spend a weekend with my family at Rishton and on alternate weekends I was invited to stay with her family who owned a butcher's shop, on Marsh House Lane at Darwen. Now Doreen had an older brother who was in the Royal Navy on HMS *Victorious*, the aircraft carrier. He was a telegrapher and we later learned that *Victorious* was at that time serving in the Pacific. When he eventually came home on leave he asked me out. He seemed so mature and handsome. He was eighteen three years older than me, and I fear my fickle feelings for Bobby flew out of the window. Tom really was a dashing young man and I was quite smitten. That leave we had a really wonderful time. Doreen partnered Tom's friend Ronnie, and the highlight of our times together was visiting a travelling fair, which had arrived at Blackburn. Sadly Tom's leave ended and he returned to his ship. Doreen and I came down to earth and were back at school. Tom and I corresponded with each other and I quickly learned that Tom really only cared for one person and that was Tom. Our friendship just seemed to fizzle out.

HMS Victorious.

Shortly afterwards my mother had a truly life-threatening illness which ultimately meant that I had to leave school prematurely, abandoning all my hopes and dreams of becoming a linguist. My older sister was by this time married with two young sons, so it was deemed necessary that I must leave school to help run the home and care for my two young sisters. In addition, with mother incapacitated, someone had to continue the business of looking after our lodgers – our only source of income.

So I moved to the family home at Rishton. I had short insignificant dates with boys I met a local 'hops' and it was whilst working as a counter clerk at Rishton Post Office I came into contact with Bill Walmsley who was a Civil Servant at Blackburn GPO. Although we had never met, a friendship gradually developed through telephone conversations. You see he would in the course of his duties, dictate telegraph messages to the Rishton sub-office which I then wrote out on telegram forms. Sealed in the then famous bright yellow envelopes they would be delivered to the addresses who lived within the postal area. Subsequently Bill invited me out to see the wrestling at King George's Hall in Blackburn. As we did not know each other we decided on a method of identification and arranged to meet – yes – under the large clock at the entrance to Blackburn Railway Station. For weeks our friendship continued. We met each Saturday and Sunday and soon learned about each other's families, hobbies and ambitions. From day one I knew there was no "spark" there for me and this was confirmed when he eventually kissed me. My concern was that he felt differently, and started to talk of getting engaged, even where we would live. I frankly explained to him that I was far too young to tie myself down and we carried on being just good friends. He even wrote to me when I joined the Land Army.

Next there was Walter, an extremely handsome man – very tall and slim with blond wavy hair and the most beautiful blue eyes. We primarily met at Tony's Ballroom in Blackburn (I first heard an electric guitar at Tony's playing the Hawaiian War Chant – wonderful!) Every Saturday night we would meet at the ballroom to dance with each other, I was not expected to partner anyone else, a bad, bad omen. We then started to go on cycle rides together when the opportunity arose. Although at sixteen I was flattered to have such a handsome boyfriend, envied by my pals, I again became bored with the same routine. In all truth Walter was a wimp, under his mother's thumb. We did continue to be pals until I joined the WLA and he also wrote to me for a while.

The relationship which caused me most concern at this time was one which I drifted into because his parents (our neighbours from Manchester) and my mother were such close friends. These ties continued even after we moved to Rishton as evacuees. Their son, Arthur, was six years older than me and it appeared to be a foregone conclusion that eventually Arthur and I would end up together. At sixteen I was footloose and fancy free an enjoying life as it was. May be he felt pressurised also but when he was getting too close I made my feelings plain. When he came home on embarkation leave prior to being sent to Egypt he asked me to write to him and wait for him. I agreed to write but once again refused to commit myself to anyone at my age. However, we enjoyed his leave together and parted on friendly terms. For a long time we corresponded regularly – I received three or four airmails or aerographs each week from him, which started by being quite platonic. In spite of my insistence that our relationship remain on a non-committal basis, his letters became more and more intimate; they graduated to how he missed me, to how much he wanted to be with me again, to how much he loved me, to how much he wanted me to be his wife. How do you write to an airman on active service, thousands of miles from home telling him that his hopes for the future were just not on? I didn't lead him on but just promised to meet him when he eventually returned home. Later he started sending gifts – a beautifully embossed leather handbag, an ornate eastern powder compact and items of jewellery and finally a ring. My reaction to the ring was a kind of guilt combined with fear of feeling trapped and this I did convey to Arthur by telling him that in no way was I prepared to wear his ring. We continued to write to each other even until the war ended in 1945 despite my many other friendships and dates with other young men.

Wounded in Action

O ur working routine at Whimple House Farm progressed. I took to the life like a duck to water especially when animals were involved. Our tasks were so varied and interesting that nobody could claim to be bored. We were learning constantly and meeting the lovely local people whose conversation we found rather difficult to comprehend due to their extremely strong West Country accents and dialogues.

As the days and weeks passed by we became more adept at milking, more confident with the pigs and cows and even the back breaking fieldwork tasks became less painful. We were unaware that the supervisor was unobtrusively making her assessment of each individual. Despite the hard graft, we had our fair share of laughter and humour. We were always singing and the camaraderie between us was unbelievable. Everything ran so smoothly; no squabbling, no jealousy and always someone ready to lend an ear and advise.

It would be about the beginning of my third week and I was ready to sit down to milk yet another cow, headscarf in place, bucket in one hand, stool in the other, when wham! All of a sudden the cow lashed out at me with its right hind leg – its hoof had caught me at the side of my right knee joint and sent me sprawling. (Well, this was the Women's Land Army wasn't it so one must expect to get wounded at some time or another)? The young herdsman sniggered but carried on with his work, it was so undignified and embarrassing! I managed to resume milking but was relieved when, work over, I limped back to the Hostel. On the morrow my knee had doubled in size and had become inflamed. The supervisor sent me to see the local GP, who confirmed that, although there was severe bruising, no serious damaged had been done, so with aspirin to ease the aches and pains I hobbled on working as usual but after a few days a series of what seemed to be boils appeared down my leg – five in number – and they were really painful. Back to the GP I went. He said they were carbuncles and advised the application of antifligistine poultices each morning. The supervisor heated up the tin of paste each morning following breakfast and when she considered it was hot enough, it was thickly spread on squares of lint forming very hot poultices. These were slapped on each carbuncle whereupon I nearly hit the ceiling – it was agony. However, the treatment succeeded but left me with five nasty scars. Whether these infections were due to the kick form the cow or whether they were purely coincidental I'll never know but that wicked, hot, grey paste certainly did the trick.

My First Real Love

Ihad been at Whimple for three or four days and was settling well into the daily routine. Half way through the week (I believe it was on Thursday) Alma and I decided to slip down to the Fountain for an hour or so. Having completed our chores for the day, washed, changed from our smelly dungarees, boots and gaiters and partaken of yet another good dinner, we strolled down the lane. On arrival the room was bursting at the seams, absolutely teeming with people.

"Let's give it a miss," I suggested before we had even bought a drink, "There's no pleasure in this." Exiting on to the lane Alma had a bright idea. "Come on, Micky, let's see what's doing at the New Inn."

For some reason, probably because it was further from the hostel, we seldom patronised the New Inn.

"Is it worth it, Alma?" I retorted, "It will be just as crowded … I think I'll call it a day."

Alma looked rather glum so I added, "Okay, let's take a look. If it's bad we can always go home."

So we strolled on through the village in the direction of the New Inn. Our luck was in for on entering we decided it was much more comfortable and whilst I went to the bar for our drinks, Alma managed to find a small table for two. I noticed that the young man who stood next to me and was already being served spoke to Alma as he passed our table and went through a door at the rear of the pub. I carried our drinks back to our table.

"Shall we go outside on the patio?" said Alma.

"I wonder why?" I said, trying to sound sarcastic, linking Alma's request with the short tête-à-tête she'd had with the good-looking young man.

"You don't miss much, do you?" she laughed.

"It's just that he says there is more room out there and it isn't so stuffy."

We passed through the rear door and out on to the patio and immediately four young US sailors who had been seated around a table jumped up simultaneously and offered us their seats. They proved to be very good company. It turned out to be a very jolly evening; laughing, joking and being entertained by one guy who I think really believed he was Bing Crosby. I did notice a subtle exchange of seats had taken place during the evening placing Al next to Alma and Stoney alongside me. Eventually

Alma glanced at her wrist watch (at that stage in my life I could not afford to buy one).

"Sorry, guys," she said, "Curfew draws nigh," and pushing back our chairs we quickly called "Goodnight everybody!" and left the New Inn.

As we walked back up the lane towards the hostel, Al and Stoney caught up with us.

"We couldn't let you walk out of our lives like this," joked Al, "This could be the start of something big!!"

Alma and I agreed later on that we had both had the same thoughts, namely, "Yea, another over-sexed, mouthy Yank," but as there was safety in numbers, we allowed the boys to escort us 'home'. Within a short distance of the entrance Alma and Al paused but Stoney and I continued on. We stopped by the wall and I bade him "Goodnight".

"Can I see you tomorrow night?" he queried and I agreed, whereupon he took both my hands in his, kissed each one in turn and then planted a short, soft kiss on my cheek.

"See, yah," he squeezed my hand, turned and strode down the lane.

I couldn't get him out of my thoughts the following day; Alma teased me about being in a daydream.

"That sure must have been some kiss," she assumed, little did she know how dispassionate a kiss it had been, yet so utterly meaningful.

As Stoney had been unsure of his duties, we had arranged to go to the New Inn the following evening to meet. Alma and Al had made their own arrangements and I remember feeling a little odd waiting there alone. The evening wore on and I was just thinking that I had been stood up when he appeared. In wartime duty held priority – we all knew that – and from the start I felt that Stoney was different for me than other guys I had met. It was not exactly love at first sight but certainly a strong, mutual attraction to each other. During our later conversations he confided to me that he felt the same way I did.... we just hated to be apart. He even admitted that whilst strolling back to the Station on the first night we met, he couldn't work out why he hadn't taken me in his arms, kissed and fondled me as he had done with previous girlfriends, particularly as Al couldn't get over what a 'good kisser' Alma was. He eventually turned up and I was quite relieved. For the remainder of the evening we sat close together on an old settle, holding hands and deep in conversation. Quietly we discussed each other's families, homes, previous employment. We bonded there and then and our eye contact was magical – it said it all.

The next four weeks flew by so quickly. We kept to our previous arrangement or meeting at the Inn although we decided to change it to the New Fountain because it was nearer the hostel. Sometimes, he would be there first according to his shift and on occasion he couldn't make it at all but I always knew he would be there if his work allowed and I invariably went down each evening to wait. If he couldn't make it one night, he would be there the next or the one after that. I was so much in love that I had no interest in attention paid me by the other boys.

Whilst waiting for him to show, I always sat in an alcove with the USAAF crewmen – sometimes three sometimes four, sometimes five. This actually came about one evening when one of them came across to my table and invited me to join him and his colleagues at their table. Thinking he was trying to 'pick me up' I thanked him kindly and explained that I was awaiting my boyfriend.

"Wait with us then," he said.

I had previously been aware of these airmen. They were conspicuous because they were the only airmen to turn up on a regular basis at the Fountain. Other clients were civilians or predominantly US sailors. I never really knew where they were stationed but thought it might have been at Exeter Airport, which was a short distance down the A30. However, they seemed more mature than our crowd – late twenties/early thirties. So I carried my shandy over to their table and we all formerly introduced ourselves. The gentleman (yes, he was a real gentleman) who had invited me over was American but of Polish descent. His name was Frank Wz....ski. He explained that he was married with two children, a little girl of four and a little boy two years older. It was obvious that he missed his family terribly and he took a photograph from his breast pocket and proudly introduced me to his adored family.

"I'll get back to them one day," he'd say. Many were the times we talked over the next couple of weeks. He loved his home and brought snapshots to show me of the family with him on a veranda or porch as he called it.

I did admire these men; they were doing such a dangerous job. We were aware that the invasion of France had begun though everything was so "hush-hush". If Frank wasn't around on the nights I joined the group to wait for Stoney I'd say, "Where's Frank?" Not a word passed their lips but they would drone, imitating a plane engine and glance up towards the ceiling then I knew he was on night sorties.

Frank himself opened his heart to me unashamedly about his fears that one day he may not come back, "Anyone who says they have no doubts about their safety is a damn liar," he would say, "Sure it's all in a nights work, I know. I am a non-believer yet when things 'hot up' up there and the flack gets too close for comfort, there's only Him and me and I pray like hell, like I've never prayed before!"

The friendship that developed with these brave men was wonderful and we continued to share our conversation whenever fate threw us together at the Fountain Inn.

It was a little after two weeks from us meeting. I went down one evening as usual and Frank wasn't there. To my usual enquiry "Where's Frank?" I was met with doleful looks and sad eyes. Nothing was said, no droning of a plane but his closest colleague simply gave me a thumbs down signal. I knew what this meant, Frank had been shot down. Immediately my heart, thoughts and tears went out for that lovely, lovely family in the USA. Poor Frank, I never knew exactly how or where he met his end but I never saw him again – ever. All I know is that I feel honoured, to this day, at having known Frank and all his brave buddies; they are all in my thoughts and prayers especially on Remembrance Day each year when I still shed tears for Frank, just as I did all those years ago on that terrible night I realised his fate.

A Regal Ride

My romance with Stoney progressed – we were so much in love and every parting was agonising. The first time we kissed was magic; the earth really did move and so it continued throughout our courtship. We were just so very happy with each other's company that no-one or nothing else mattered. Luckily we managed to meet about five times each week and on weekdays when we had to be up early for duty, we remained at Whimple, taking a stroll through the lovely countryside or meeting up with the others at the public houses, but at weekends with later curfew we would meet at the entrance lobby at Central Station at Exeter. He was fascinated by our English pubs especially the old fashioned ones which sported a piano and where everybody joined in with a singsong.

Occasionally we would brave the long queues to see a film, visit the American "Do-nut Dugout" for a doughnut and coffee, or drop into the Allied Services Club where we could have snack and play darts or table tennis in the sports and pastimes section which was on the first floor of the Club. He always travelled back with me to Whimple on the train to ensure I got back 'home' safely. Even on Wednesday evenings, when we Land Girls were obliged to stay in and watch ENSA, he would come out, meet me after the show at the garden gate just to hold me for a few minutes and kiss me 'Goodnight' before my curfew.

I must tell you about an incident that happened one Saturday. Alma and I had pre-arranged to meet Al and Stoney in Exeter. We had worked until mid-day and having quickly washed and donned our smart breeches, hacking jackets and sexy hats, we decided for a change to go by bus. This time we had to walk up the lane until we reached the A30 junction and crossing the road we awaited the bus at the designated bus stop. We had been there but a few minutes when a huge, smart black car pulled in alongside the grass verge and stopped. The middle-aged driver, or should I say chauffeur as he was in immaculate uniform, alighted and asked if we intended going into Exeter.

"Yes, we're actually waiting to catch the bus which is due," we informed him. Whereupon he held open the rear door of the car as he offered us a lift. He probably noticed Alma and I give a suspicious glance at each other for he explained that this wonderful automobile belonged to Queen

Wilhelmena of the Netherlands who was at that time in exile and residing in England having fled Holland when it had been overrun by the Germans. With this he indicated to the Royal Dutch coat of arms on the door. It seemed that he had been instructed to offer transport to anyone in uniform providing he was not diverted from the pre-arranged route. Reassured, we thanked him and climbed into the car. What a magnificent vehicle it was! We thought it very impressive from the outside but inside it was the height of luxury. The veneered panelling and cocktail bar is still impressed in my memory. A lift in any car would have been considered a luxury because with petrol rationing cars were few and far between but to be afforded a ride in this one made an undying impression on my mind. We truly did have something to boast about when we returned to the Hostel later that evening!

On the Move Again

In accordance with the usual routine, after two weeks training, six girls left to take up their permanent posts in agriculture and my co-trainees and I became "seniors" showing the ropes to the six girls who had arrived during the weekend at the commencement of their training. This made little change to our daily working routine. I was both pleased and amazed to meet up again with one of the newcomers. She was called Kathy and we had previously met at the recruitment centre in Blackburn weeks earlier whilst being interviewed after volunteering.

Then two weeks later it was time for the five of us to move on. Prior to proceeding to our designated farms we were given leave. We finished work on the Friday afternoon but remained at Whimple House that night, leaving early on Saturday morning. Supervisor summoned us to the lounge one last time after dinner on Friday.

"Now girls as you are aware, your training here is complete and you are allowed two days leave, Saturday and Sunday. Anyone who wishes is entitled to go home for the two days but I see that your homes are so far way that this would be impossible. I have therefore arranged for all five of you to stay in a boarding house in Exeter from dinnertime tomorrow evening until after breakfast on Monday morning – breakfast will be at 8am enabling you to make an early start to your prospective farms."

With this she handed to each of us an envelope.

"Inside is your pay to date and travel pass. Also inside are your individual instructions as to how you will be met and the name and address of your future employer. I only hope that the knowledge (if any) you have gained here will be put to good use. I repeat yet again that no two farms are alike and it is up to you to fall in with the systems and routines in progress wherever you are sent. Well done, girls, and good luck."

With this we were dismissed.

Throughout our training supervisor had been helpful, supportive and appreciative of our efforts. The girls who passed through Whimple House came from all walks of life – many leaving behind luxurious, comfortable homes and well paid cushy jobs with high expectancy of career promotions and this laborious work came hard too many. Later I discovered that the conditions even here were like being in heaven compared to what we had to face in the future. Yes, supervisor had been very fair in all aspects, listening to any problems we met with and showing us the respect we showed her, yet she insisted we keep to the rules such as precision timekeeping, enforcing the curfew and demanding our best efforts at all times workwise.

Hurriedly we packed all our personal belongings that evening, said our final farewells to our other Land Girl friends and to the friends we had made at the New Fountain Inn and all decided on an early night.

Stoney was there at the Inn as usual. He was aware that I would be moving on and was quite concerned as to where it would be.

"Micky," he said, "Let's go over to the New Inn tonight, It's kinda rowdy here."

We walked down through the Square arms around each other, sneaking an occasional kiss as we strolled on. It was much quieter at the New Inn and we managed to get a small table in one corner of the lounge. He was greatly relieved to learn that my posting was at Honiton, just a couple of train stops along the line.

That evening we discussed the future for the first time. We even talked of staying together for the weekend but despite the great temptation decided to abandon the idea. How could we make plans or even take risks when life in general was so uncertain? He had never betrayed the orders he had received with regards to the location of his barracks or station or what went on there and I never thought of asking. That was the way it was in these unpredictable times – I was aware of the invasion of Normandy and guessed he could be sent away at any time without notice.

He told me yet again that he was deeply in love with me and, taking his Navy ring from his finger, he placed it on the third finger of my left hand. He held it there for some time before taking his hand away. "Micky, we don't know what the future holds. We don't even know if there'll be a future but please wear this for me and one day, God willing, I'll come back and replace it with a real one."

It felt loose and floppy on my finger but to me it looked so beautiful. In actual fact it was a man's ring, a heavy silver signet ring with the black stone inscribed "US Navy" and I wore it whenever it was practical from that day onwards, taking it off when I was sure I'd never see Stoney again and on the occasion I met the man who would later become my husband. I passed it on to the gentleman who gave me away on the eve of my wedding.

Goodbye Whimple

Five of us left Whimple House together on Saturday morning laden with suitcases and various other items of luggage and arrived in Exeter mid-morning. We hadn't a clue where our lodgings were situated and Exeter centre had been virtually flattened with the bombing so we decided to make use of taxis. On reading the address we handed to him on a slip of paper the taxi driver immediately set off, obviously well aware where we needed to go. Although we were not allowed access to our rooms until later that afternoon, a maid advised us to leave our luggage in the lobby and having do so, we all trouped out again and meandered back to the city centre. We had coffee together before going our separate ways. Alma and I decided to do some shopping having recently received our wage packets. Incidentally, whilst at Whimple we were paid 17/6d per week (this works out at 87? pence in today's currency). We had our board and lodgings, of course, and our uniforms and although the wages paid are relative to the times it was still poor pay. Our shopping proved to be a bit of a hit and miss effort, most shops being heaps of rubble and, in any case we had no clothing coupons. We managed to purchase a few toiletries, writing paper and envelopes and a few postage stamps. We than snacked at the Allied Services Club and made our way back to our lodgings, where we were shown our room and decided to take a cat-nap.

We freshened up on awakening and after a somewhat frugal meal (what a shock after the delicious food we had sampled at Whimple House) it was time for us to meet Al and Stoney. That evening was spent in a crowded, little back street pub, which sported a piano and a good pianist and a whole lot of hilarity. We had a good old-time sing-a-long. The boys were highly amused but then they got the hang of it, joined in and after a thoroughly enjoyable evening they delivered us back to our lodgings, lingering on the doorstep until the ultimate minute of the ten o'clock curfew. Before leaving Stoney asked me to be ready for 10.30 the next morning as he had a surprise for me.

It was after 10.30 when we managed to get away the next day which, of course, was Sunday, due to the fact that this small boarding house was funded by a religious charity and the elderly landlady was, we discovered, very, very religious. So after breakfast (porridge and toast) it was compulsory to attend a religious service which went on and on. When it finally ended we were advised that Sunday curfew was 9.30. I was relieved to get out into the sunlight – the rooms there were so dark and dismal, the atmosphere quite Victorian.

I had racked my brain trying to surmise what my surprise was going to be and now I was about to find out. In actual fact Stoney, Al and another one of his buddies (who was also courting Margery, one of our group) had booked with the Sports and Activities Division of the Allied Services Club for a horse riding session for themselves and their girlfriends! We were taken to the outskirts of Exeter where there were huge stables. Here we were lectured on the care of a horse, the hazards of horse riding, the grooming and the harnessing and unharnessing of the animals. I remember very little of the actual ride, save for the fact that it was a completely new experience for us city dwellers. US sailors astride a horse did not somehow look quite right, in fact the sight of them, all as inexperienced as we were, was hilarious. Not one of us had ever ridden before and despite the fun, we all ended up very, very saddle sore.

It was difficult arranging our next meeting. The situation was so very uncertain. I was unaware as to when I would have any free time in my new job. We were entitled to one half day each week plus Sunday. We had, however, been warned that cows have to be milked seven days a week, our services might be required on Sundays but that all time worked over forty-two hours was subject to overtime pay. Before Stoney left me that Sunday evening we made provisional plans to meet in Honiton the following Saturday evening. I gave him my new address – I never knew his – and we parted dejectedly.

On Monday morning we were all up very early and buzzing with excitement; we were also scared. Five of us had lived together, slept in one room, shared each other's clothes and make-up, set each others hair, worked together, dined together, laughed together, sang together and confided in each other over the past four weeks; we were one big happy family and now we were to split up being sent "God knows where"!

Grace was said before we tucked into a reasonable breakfast, then with the exception of Margery, who was a Jewess, we were asked to attend a short service. After that came hugs and tears as we went our separate ways. WE had all been issued with travel warrants. Three girls were off to North Devon, one to the South Hams and I was to retrace my journey but then on past Whimple to Honiton.

Ruth and I had a short interval before our trains were due in at Central Station and so we bought a coffee and carried it over to the usual corner in the Allied Services Club. We had to share a table with two other girls unknown to us.

"Have you been assigned to your farms?" one of these girls asked.

"Yes," said Ruth and read out the address.

"And where are you off to?" the other girl addressed me.

"To Honiton" I replied.

"Oh I was near Honiton until two weeks ago," she said, "It was horrendous and the boss was a real slave driver," she continued, "Stuck it for just two weeks and walked out."

"Where are you now?" queried Ruth.

"Working in a gang at Honiton – much easier. Whereabouts in Honiton are you going?" she turned to me.

Referring to my instructions I read out, "Mr and Mrs Edwards, Kitts Farm, Upottery."

She gasped, open mouthed, "That's where I was, oh no! Sorry," she gulped, "Hope I haven't put you off. I'll keep my mouth shut."

No other reference was made to my new position and it wasn't long before she said her "Goodbye" and left hurriedly.

I remained there for some time in complete shock. What a prospect! AT that point in time my future seemed very uncertain.

Yet orders were orders and I had mine, I was to catch the train to Honiton Railway Station where my future employer's wife would meet me. No special identification was deemed necessary, as obviously I would be in Land Army Uniform.

I caught the appropriate train and during its brief pause at Whimple Station a wave of nostalgia swept over me. But then it was soon on its way again into what I considered to be the great unknown.

The Great Unknown

As I stepped down from the train on to the platform at Honiton Station I immediately knew Mrs Edwards – it was so obvious that she was there to meet someone and from her querulous glances she wasn't sure whom. Relief fleetingly crossed her face as she perceived my Women's Land Army uniform and she strolled over to meet me.

After mutual introductions we proceeded up New Street and then left down a blustery High Street to the bus stop by the Three Tuns public house. The journey to Upottery was endured in awkward silence. It did give me chance to make a rough assessment of this little lady with whom I was destined to spend my immediate future. On first meeting her I had surmised she was a "little old lady". Her attire was very old fashioned albeit of excellent cut and quality and the brimmed felt hat did nothing to flatter her lovely face. And then I realised she was by no means old, in fact, she was barely middle aged. Her skin was pale and somewhat sallow but I later learned that she was experiencing health problems which would account for this. I later found out that in this community, any make-up was considered sort of corrupting and her very dark straight hair enhanced the pallor of her skin.

It was quite a distance from Devonshire Inn Farm, where we had alighted, to Kitts Farm. We went so far along the A30, turned left under Bob Shutes Cover and left again down Kitts Lane which was rough and steep. I was quite heavily laden with all my worldly possessions and Mrs Edwards carried a shopping bag and handbag in one hand and recently charged wireless accumulator in the other.

When we eventually reached the farm I was completely overwhelmed by the beauty of the surrounding countryside. The farm was perched quite high on a hillside overlooking the beautiful valley – the Otter Valley – the fields sloped gently down to the River Otter and then upwards to a copse on the crest of the opposite hill. This vista stretched before me from north to south as far as the eye could see, with the river, like a ribbon, meandering its twisting journey to the sea through this verdant countryside sparsely dabbed with farms and cottages. It was the most picturesque scenery I had seen hitherto in my short life.

Before entering the farmhouse we traversed a small trickling brook by

The beautiful Otter Valley.

means of a large granite slab. Through a door we passed entering a wash-house or outhouse with red brick floor, large copper boiler and at the top end was a pipe from which water trickled into a kettle hanging from it. A large zinc bath captured the overflow. Leading from the wash-house was the door into the kitchen and what a jumble this appeared to be! Open shelving running the length of the kitchen housed all kinds of utensils and products – jars of goose grease, next to cattle drenches plus a hollow cows horn (used for administering the treatments), next to beeswax, next to ointment for warble fly, next to a plate with butter, next to a bag of sugar and so on. Beneath these shelves was a large wooden table covered with oilcloth containing a couple of chipped enamel washing up bowls and an enamel tray where pots were draining. Other pots and cooking utensils littered the remaining space on the table. There was no sign of a sink with taps but there was a contraption which I later learned was an oil cooker. (From time to time and without reason or warning this paraffin stove would flare up, filling the room with smoke and black, oily, sooty particles).

A doorway lead from the kitchen to the living room; the ceilings were very low and smoke dyed and the floors throughout were of concrete, worn shiny, with several rough patches where repairs had been carried out. In the far corner of the room was an inglenook fireplace. This consisted of a pair of huge firedogs standing on a stone slab with a huge log extending horizontally across. Beneath the log were ashes and the remaining pieces of small wood. The wall behind was black with what appeared to be solidified tar. A metal bar traversed the fireplace and from this hung vertical rods hooked at the bottom from which hung a blackened kettle. A wooden bench ran from the rear wall in towards the room on each side so that when seated there, one could look straight up the chimney where two hams hung, being smoked. A large black oak beam spanned the chimney breast to which was attached a shallow shelf. Above the left hand bench was an iron door opening up into a bread oven.

The remaining furniture consisted of a big, oil-clothed covered dining table, an even larger veneered wooden table, a Victorian sideboard with mirrors, an occasional table beneath one window, four wooden dining chairs, a carver chair, a really tatty easy chair whereupon a Spaniel snoozed, and another old easy chair. The polished table was huge stretching along the whole length of one wall and it held a motley of items – stacks of papers, Pullman's Weekly News and Farmers Weekly, letters, invoices, pens and pencils, cheque books and bank drafts, a large wireless, in fact everything "bar the kitchen sink" was strewn from one end to the other haphazardly. There were two small windows, one overlooked the front garden, brook and lane and the other one overlooked an overgrown vegetable plot at the rear of the house. Several candles in chipped enamel holders stood on the sideboard. These holders had an integrated tray with a fingerloop and each tray carried a box of matches. A single wick oil lamp with tall glass funnel took pride of place amongst the candleholders. There was no sign of electricity, no wall switches, no lights! To say that this was a real culture shock would be putting it mildly. Although I had come from a working class background, our home had all modern conveniences and comforts such as hot and cold water on tap, electricity, up-to-date electric cooker, lovely, large bathroom with porcelain bath, washbasin and flush toilet. Our dining room boasted a large cast iron and tile grate which gleamed from being blackleaded with Zebo, always warm and welcoming with a roaring fire and an extremely efficient oven alongside from whence lovely odours of home cooking permeated the room.

Mrs Edwards lifted the latch of a wooden door and pulling it towards her she proceeded to climb a flight of bare wooden stairs. I followed. We turned left at the top and followed a long passage to the opposite end of the house passing three bedroom doors. Finally she indicated the last door and we passed through it into a fairly large bedroom. Possibly it appeared large to me because it was so bare – the floor was of rough wooden boards – no linoleum or carpets – just a frayed and tatty piece of coconut matting placed alongside the bed. Again, as throughout the house the ceilings were low and the single small window which overlooked the hayshed and orchard was set part in the wall and part in the sloping ceiling. All the doors were wooden tongue and grooved and all had large metal latches.

"I'll leave you here now to unpack. Come down when you're ready," I was told, "Dinner is always at one o'clock unless something drastic happens," she said. Then as an afterthought, "By the way, there is a chamber pot under your bed for the night. Unless it's really necessary I wouldn't advise using the lavatory during the night. Apart from it being a route march there are lots of rats around there during the dark hours."

With this she turned and left the room leaving me completely gobsmacked. I had never, ever, been in such a cold, dark, dismal room. The double iron bedstead looked far from inviting (it was less inviting still when that evening I threw back the bedding to discover that the mattress consisted of two tightly packed straw palliases and it felt like I was lying on concrete. There was quite a ridge where the two palliases met and it took me weeks to adjust to sleeping in such discomfort.

An old chest of drawers was situated corner-wise at one end of the room with a couple of knob handles missing and a worm eaten washstand stood corner-wise at the other side. This held a chipped enamel basin which slotted into a cut out hole on the top shelf. Below was another shelf also forming a shallow drawer and this contained a saucer with a tablet of White Windsor soap. Yes under the bed was the chamberpot and above the chest hung a wooden framed, mottled mirror. The only other piece of furniture was an old wooden chair next to the bedhead.

For a few minutes my gaze wandered back and forth around the room contemplating how I could make anything vaguely resembling warmth and homeliness out of this room. It was basically clean but the décor was stained and depressing. The walls were distempered in a dismal, depressing shade of green and the gloss paintwork was the colour of mud – a yucky shade of brown. I later learnt that every room in the house with the exception of the two family bedrooms were in exactly the same colours. Apparently the Viscount Sidmouth owned the entire village and these were the standard paints used in every house, cottage and farm unless, of course, the tenants saw fit to spend out money and internally decorate their dwellings privately, but most did not!

I sat down on the bed in near despair and the conversation I'd had that very morning with the previous land girl flooded my mind. Surely there was nowhere in England without a bathroom, a flush toilet and electricity. Obviously there was!

I carefully unpacked my suitcase etc. and placed everything in the drawers. I had a good supply of my own toiletries which went alongside the soap saucer, and my scant items of make-up were put on top of the chest, I threw my pyjamas on my pillow and changed into my aertex shirt and dungarees. Although the small window had no curtains, nobody would have been able to see me because the glass was too mucky.

Then I retraced my steps downstairs and noticed that the fire had been lit and standing on a kind of trivet amongst the ashes was a large pan steaming away. "I'm sorry, maid," said Mrs Edwards, "But we'll have to take pot luck for dinner today – haven't had time to do much and father will be in at one – he always likes his dinner on time." "Sit down, but I'll tell 'ee that there's fathers' chair," she remarked pointing to the one and only easy chair.

As there was nothing at hand save the hard wooden dining chairs, I plumped for the hard wooden bench within the inglenook and squirmed there until one o'clock.

True to prediction Mr Edwards came in at precisely one o'clock wearing thick woollen socks having discarded his boots in the outhouse. He threw his tatty tweed cap, frisbee fashion, across the room and it came to rest on the table beneath the window.

As he walked diagonally across the room towards me his hand was out-stretched ready to clasp mine in a warm handshake and I was struck by the gentle, pale blue eyes, ruddy complexion and tousled faded ginger hair.

"Thees got yer then, maid?" he retorted – part statement, part question.

Not waiting for an answer he beckoned for me to sit at the top end of the table. His wife then carried in a large bowl of boiled potatoes, quite a large joint of boiled beef (left from the previous day) onions and carrots, in a thick, rich gravy.

Mr Edwards carved the beef in thick, tempting slices, the like of which I had never been served with before. "God helps them as helps themselves, maid, so dig in." It was a wonderful meal and I watched as he smoothed lashings of Coleman's Mustard across his own beef slices. Mrs Edwards carried away the dirty dishes and returned with bowls of deep, home-made apple pie heaped up with home-made clotted cream.

Throughout my working life at Kitts Farm the standard of food remained constantly high – not luxurious or pretentious but good, plain wonderful home grown home-cooked produce.

I suppose it was just as well that the meals were so nutritious because, my goodness, the work was hard and the hours were long and every ounce was needed. During the meal husband and wife, conversed with each other in a very, strong West Country dialect occasionally including me but I didn't understand a word that was said which they thought very amusing.

Having already changed into my working clothes I was prepared to begin the rounds of the farm with Mr Edwards.

My Future Domain

I followed Mr Edwards down the lane, along the front of the farmhouse and, turning left, entered a courtyard (farmyard) through large double gates. These opened inwards onto the yard. Forty per cent of the area was completely taken over by a huge, tall dung heap. On the lower side there was just enough space between the dung heap and a cowshed to get through. Khaki green sludge oozed from the base out over the cobbles to a concrete gutter, which carried it away. I thought to myself how disgusting this was and made a mental note that, if I had any say in the matter, this dung heap had to be carted out for the fields for spreading as a priority and the yard completely cleaned.

Just within the double galvanised metal gates and situated on the left was what Mr Edwards called a chattrelle, or a large trough hewn from stone (Mr Edwards always referred to the water trough as the chattrelle and sheds for sheltering animals were linneys). It was approximately 4 feet long by 2½ feet wide by 2½ feet deep. The overflow of spring water serving the house was channelled down into this trough so there was a constant overflow into a grid. This cold, clean, running water had many uses.

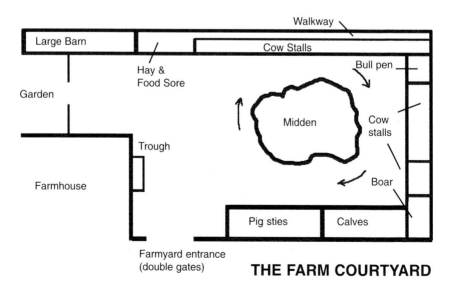

THE FARM COURTYARD

The domestic gardens and the end of the house formed the higher boundary of the yard. Farm buildings and sheds formed the other three sides thus forming a quadrangle. As we trailed around the buildings Mr Edwards pointed out their various uses.

Firstly I was introduced to the bull. He was a gigantic animal – beefy, large framed and high on legs with a wide, huge head which he shook periodically as he snorted causing a slimy mucus to drip from the large metal ring in his nose. My boss explained that he was quite old, had become ill tempered (through age) and was really due for replacement when the next Bull Sale came around at Exeter.

He really looked to be a powerful beast and obviously a pure bred Devon Red. Mr Edwards explained that he chose this breed because the progeny were good, beefy animals whilst at the same time having a decent lactation. He also explained that he had currently between 24 to 30 dairy cows plus yearlings, calves, heifers (maiden) and in calf heifers. But of course, I realised that, being a fairly small mixed farm, other animals were to be cared for too, even though my primary occupation would be the welfare of the herd.

I had little to do for the small flock of sheep. I think they had been bought as young stock for fattening and not for breeding. I say this because I never came across a ram or lambs but we did take them to a neighbouring farm where there was a sheep dip and Mr Edwards had the assistance of contract shearers for that purpose even though he was quite adept at the task. My only contact with them was when they needed to be moved. They were out to graze requiring supplementary feeding of hay and sheep nuts during the bad weather and when being prepared for market. When they were deemed to be of the correct weight we had the difficult task of weighing them for selection for market. The most difficult part was catching them. They would be herded into the courtyard for this purpose and it took three of us to catch each sheep – round and round the dung heap they would run whilst we made efforts to grab them. On more than one occasion I have grabbed a hind leg only to have fallen full length in the muck as the sheep made a sudden bolt for it. But no matter what I always hung on. Then we would place a sack slingwise under the sheep's belly then hook it onto large spring balances. For some considerable time they would bleat, kick and squirm but eventually when they calmed down, we would read the scales.

Just two Large White Sows were kept for breeding and at that time one had a nice sized litter. There was also a vicious old boar (the bane of my life along with the bull.)

One shed housed a couple of young calves, which were let out to suckle until we weaned them. After this preliminary tour of the farmyard, Mr Edwards ushered me through the gates and across the lane to a row of stone

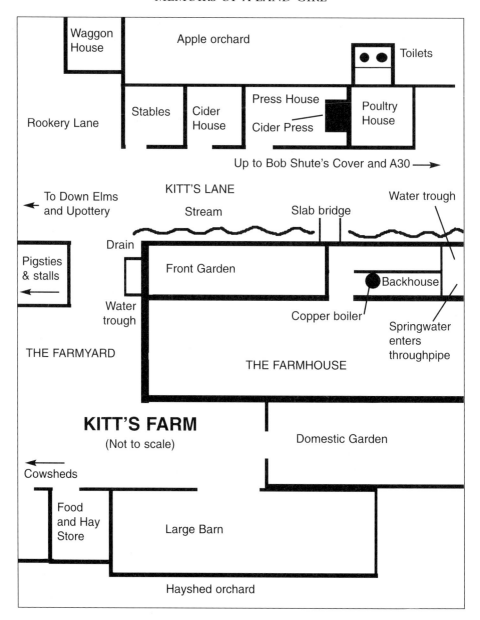

KITT'S FARM
(Not to scale)

built buildings below which was situated the wagon house which housed several items of agricultural machinery, e.g. Horserake, tedder, plough all with horse hitches. We didn't have anything mechanised – no car. No tractor, no engines of any kind. All field work was carried out manually or by working huge Shire horses. The wagon house also held a wagon with lades folded down and a grotty old putt with no sides, back or front. It was virtually a sturdy platform with a wheel at each side and a pair of shafts which rested on the ground. Later I was advised that it originally had deep sides but those days were obviously long gone. I distinctly remember looking at it trying to puzzle out to what purpose it could be put. It turned out to be the means of transporting tools and/or materials (and often me) to whichever part of the farm we needed to work on – a kind of poor man's taxi. I grew to love that old putt!

On entering the lower stone building, which turned out to be the stables, I was introduced to 'Bob', a medium sized very dark brown mare. Bob turned out to have a very unpredictable nature and at times refused point blank to work or even move when the mood took her. There were three empty stalls alongside Bob and all had large, slatted hay racks high on the wall with a feeding trough below. A horizontal hitching post was fixed alongside each partition wall. On the end wall hung the harnesses and tack. Mr Edwards explained that Bob had just been brought in from work and that there were two other mares out in the paddock. Frolic was an old breeding mare, light tan in colour with white face markings. I was told that she had a mind of her own and her favourite means of showing her displeasure was to give an unexpected and crafty nip. But all the time I worked her we got on famously – she would do anything I asked of her. I never knew exactly how old she was but features, physique and mainly teeth intimated she was very old, indeed, she never produced another foal. Her last and ultimate offspring was Pansy, our other mare. I believe she was about four years old, and a really beautiful young horse. She had almost identical markings to Frolic but was of far greater stature – a truly magnificent, proud horse who proved to be the hardest worker of all three. She never refused what was asked of her workwise and she was very affectionate towards me, always trying to nuzzle into my face. I loved her dearly. One flaw to her temperament was that she was scared of 'planes and cars. This was wartime and rural England so cars were not too great a problem but in the area three wartime airfields were situated with runways of course. They were at Dunkeswell (US Navy) Smeathorpe (RAF) and Tickney Warren (coloured US base) – so it was inevitable that on many occasions planes flew overhead at a very low altitude. In addition there were also the odd enemy aircraft passing over on a bombing mission. Whenever I heard the distant drone of a plane be it friend or foe, I immediately had to grasp the reins tightly to the bit on either side of her mouth and hang on like grim death. Most times Pansy, in fear, would rear up high on her back legs and gosh! what a formidable sight she was. Hanging on tightly she would take me up off my feet with her before we came down to ground again. I always swung my feet and legs away from her as she landed, wary that should she land on my feet, they would be smashed to smithereens. This method would invariably keep her under control and once the offending machine had passed she immediately reverted to her old gentle self again. I sometimes watched her in the field when a plane flew overhead. Then, with nobody to control and calm her, she would rear "sky high" and on landing she would bolt as far as she could.

Leaving the stables, we proceeded up the lane and through the next door – this was the cider house where the cider was stored in huge barrels or hogs heads. They were placed alongside each other right around the room lying on their sides with trigs keeping them in place. All were sealed with the exception of the one nearest the door. This one was tapped so the cider could be easily obtainable for consumption. Mr Edwards explained that newly pressed cider was placed in a hogs head with an open bung to allow fermentation and when all the impurities had frothed out it could then be sealed. "Have a taste, maid," he offered, "Tell me what you think." I was no connoisseur on drink of any kind but I took the proffered earthenware mug and took a swig. Surprisingly I found it quite a pleasant drink despite the grubby state of the mug and the thoughts going through my brain as to how many people had used the mug before me without it having been washed.

"Like it maid?"

"I sure do," I replied.

"It's there any time you feel like a swig, help yerself," he offered.

"Thank you sir," I countered as I took the mug up to the water trough and washed it as well as I could.

"My father saved cider made in a good year when he was younger which I still keep and it's stronger than any whiskey," he explained.

"Now we'll go next door and show you where it's made." With this we entered the next building I had noticed a firm, permanent stair-like ladder firmly secured to the ground and leading to a loft above this building, but below on the ground floor was an ancient, solid oak square cider press.

"In a few weeks' time we will be working with this," he pointed to the press, "So one of my priorities is to prepare the equipment and hogs heads, in fact, we'll do that next week."

Out on the lane once more he indicated to the last building which was a hen house. Apparently this was his wife's domain – poultry. Her interest was poultry of every kind – hens, ducks and geese, and this was shared with their young daughter, Gladys, who was attending the secondary school in Honiton.

I was relieved to learn that this was their hobby and that my services would not be required as far as the poultry was concerned – it was not my favourite sphere in farming.

There was a gate adjoining this last building affording entrance to a large orchard, which sloped steeply to a gully. Built on to the back of the poultry shed were the toilets. Enclosed in a lean-to they were virtually wooden enclosures of two "pits", the boards across were at two heights, one presumably for children and one for adults, and the horizontal seats had a round hole cut into the centre of each. The edges of these holes were smoothed down to a levelled finish, whether purposely so, or whether the results of years of bottoms continually sliding on and off. The smell was putrid despite Mr Edwards occasionally throwing in lime and Mrs Edwards scattering ashes within from time to time. Whole sheets of newspaper were within reach for use as toilet paper (I never stayed in there long enough to read them for fear of the rats). From time to time the boss manually emptied the pits but this was a task I was not expected to perform, thank goodness!

"Well maid, that'll be enough to be going on with," said the boss, "The rest I'll explain day to day as we go on."

"We'll go down lower orchard now and see how 'ole Roy is getting on, he's supposed to be picking up apples."

'Ole Roy turned out to be a young man eighteen or nineteen years old. As he was unfit for National Service due to deafness and chest troubles, he had to share his labour between his fathers' smallholding and Kitts Farm.

He also helped out whenever possible on his Uncle Sam's pig farm near Luppitt. I have very happy memories of Roy, he was such a gentle soul, never lost his temper in any situation and he would do anything for me. He was like a brother and I was very fond of him. Sadly, when the war ended he bought a motorbike and lost his life in a terribly tragic accident on the A30 just above the farm.

As we entered the orchard gate there was a rustling movement and the branches of an apple tree swayed violently and out dropped Roy, crash onto the earth.

"What's ee doin, lad?" called Mr Edwards.

"I didna think that branch would give way like that," says Roy, scrambling to his feet, brushing himself off and discarding the offending, snapped off branch.

"Well thee's 'sposed to be pickin up apples from ground not climbing up trees." (It appeared Mr Edwards preferred "fallers" for his cider making to ensure the correct stage of ripeness). All the apples in the lower orchard were cider apples.

For the rest of the afternoon I was given the task alongside Roy of picking up apples in a galvanised bucket, then transferring them to the hessian sacks and carrying them up to the gate. Despite the good apple harvest with a glut of fruit, we managed to clear all the "fallers" that afternoon.

I returned to the farmyard whilst Roy carried the full sacks of apples up the lane, up the ladder, emptying them in the loft above the cider house. His hours completed for that day, Roy whisked off home on his bike.

Mr Edwards was pottering around in the farmyard and barn. He showed me the measure and amount of pigmeal to be fed to the sow plus her off-spring and for the old boar.

"Now, maid, when you open door to the boar's shed, run in fast, drop his food bucket and pick up the empty one and get out as fast as you can."

The questions turning in my mind were soon answered because this boar was gigantic with tusks protruding from each side of his mouth and the minute he heard the rattle of the door latch, he set up a terrible racket – part grunt and part squeal. Courageously I ran in, searching out the empty bucket in the dim light, I dropped the full one, picked up the empty one and dashed out. The boar chased me just as long as I held the bucket containing his meal but, of course, he lost interest in me as he slurped up his supper greedily. What an undignified way to feed a pig! I was rather apprehensive when I next had to feed the sow, who was squealing loudly knowing it was her turn next. As I opened the door to her sty outwards, she almost fell out on top of me. She had obviously climbed part way up the door with her forelegs and as I opened it, out she came. She was quite a gentle soul really her two interests being her litter of baby piglets and the food. She did not appear threatening in any way so I calmly poured her pigmeal which I'd mixed with water into a long, metal trough and left her to it. I did make a mental note that the sty needed a really good clean out.

Feeding and watering these animals was my daily responsibility along with William (and later Ferdinand), the bulls. The boar, however, was due for slaughter so my acquaintance with him did not last long.

Why is it that the male of the species have to be so much more ferocious than the female? The boar, the bull and even the gander caused me problems form time to time as he threatened me with his hiss, his outstretched neck and his flapping wings. I held him in awe at first but soon called his bluff and gave him as good as I got. I guess he was only protecting his females after all, even so most visitors to the farm gave him a wide berth.

"Tea time," called Mr Edwards, and we both ambled up the lane towards the house having brushed off our boots by the outside water trough. Once again the food was wholesome and delicious – home-made cheese, home cured and cooked ham, bread and butter (real 'hand turned' butter) home made jam, clotted cream and cake. Where was the rationing I had been accustomed to in civilian life?!

Gladys, their daughter, took tea with us. Invariably Gladys was referred to as "pert" whilst I was "maid" or "Mick". I was introduced to Gladys and initially she was quite shy. But soon we were getting on really well. She had quite a lot of homework to complete and that, combined with her duties in helping her mother with the poultry, filled her evenings.

After taking our fill it was time to have the dairy herd in for milking. Now every field had a name. For example there was Ham, Longmead, Leys, Leyfield, Pitfield, Higher Rookery Mead, Lower Rookery Mead, Coochy field, Roundabout, and so on. This identification of each field was very useful. It took me a little while to learn which field was which so at this initial moment of ignorance I was just directed to a third gate on the left along the lane. With the assistance of Watch, a quiet, gentle collie and her brother Towser, boisterous and aggressive, we herded the cattle back along the lane and into the courtyard from whence they each glided into their allotted stall. Walking alongside each one I quickly tethered them by slipping a T-bar through a ring on the chain around their necks and left them chewing their cud whilst I went in search of the grooming tackle. I searched each and every building without success, I couldn't even find a dairy with the necessary cooling plant and when I enquired as to their whereabouts Mr Edwards burst out laughing. Eventually it turned out there was none!

"Look ye, maid," he said, "If the udders are very mucky there's a rag on the top of the 'chattrelle'." (I have tried to find this word "chattrelle" or "shattrell" in dictionaries without success, I can only assume it was a word used and passed down in this part of the country from generation to generation.)

This water trough had so many uses. Primarily it was the sole water system for the whole of the farmyard. A constant flow of water streamed through it entering by a water pipe at one end and an outlet at the opposite side so that the trough was always full of fresh, clean water. It's main purpose of course, was to supply all the livestock with drinking water. It was used for cleaning purposes eg. swilling down the cowsheds and courtyard. When we had milked a cow we carried the milk in pails to milk churns situated in front of the trough. These were always prepared by Mrs Edwards who, having removed the lids, placed a metal sieve containing special paper filters, over the top rim of the churn, previously covered by a pure white cloth strainer. We then poured the freshly produced milk into this sieve. As and when the churn was filled, the complete sieve was transferred to the next churn and the paper filters replaced. This milk was wonderful – sweet, rich, creamy and full of flavour. The lid would be replaced on each filled churn and when all the milking had been completed, Mr Edwards and I together swung these churns up and over into the "chattrelle" to cool. Most times we got a ducking as the churn displaced the water which gushed out over the rim. Surplus churns of milk were rolled up to the trough situated outside the outhouse. Last but not least, many is the time when, dripping with sweat from slaving in the hayfields, I have submerged the whole of my head in the soft, cool, refreshing water.

Searching for the grooming cloth I eventually discovered it on an old, battered upturned galvanised bucket placed over the drain. It was stained "cow muck green" and probably contaminated the cows' udders rather than cleaning them. Within a short time of my arrival that filthy rag was replaced with more appropriate cloths plus a block of hard carbolic soap for hand washing. So much for all our lessons in milk recording and grooming we had been taught at Whimple!

On returning to the large, long cowshed I took stock of my charges and what a motley lot they looked. The herd was a mixture of several breeds. Predominantly they were Devon Reds, the boss's favourite breed, and these were interspersed with Ayrshire's and Shorthorns, one Red Poll (hornless) one white-faced Hereford and one Jersey, this latter cow included to ensure maintenance of fat content of the total milk yield. Of course, there was no milk recording as I had been led to expect during my training.

In answer to my query regarding this, Mr Edwards said, "I knows which cows give most milk and which have poor yields without writin' it down." So that was that. It was a pretty simply straightforward system of having the cows in, milking them and turning them out to grass again. Of course, during lying in time during bad weather we fed round hay and high quality straw, ground roots (mangolds) mixed with our own grown, ground corn and the cows producing the most milk were allowed a ration of dairy nuts.

At this time we had about thirty cows in milk in addition to any stock – maiden heifers, yearlings, calves and steers etc. All the diary cows were milked manually by myself, and the boss although on occasion Mrs Edwards would come out to help.

On my way back from turning out the cows that evening I paused and leaning on the gate, once more gazed out across this magnificent valley. I felt so totally relaxed and at peace as I surveyed the panoramic scene before me.

The beautiful belt of dark green trees really enhanced the summit of the hill facing me and the sun slowly set behind them. And so I made my way back to the farmhouse and to the people therein who were to become my very dear friends. No, more then friends – family.

To say the farmhouse was austere would be putting it mildly. Accustomed as I was to modern conveniences and comforts, I could never truly come to terms with the dowdiness of the place but the people therein made everything bearable and worthwhile. During my years spent there Mr Edwards was like the father I had never known, caring and protective, although I always referred to my employer and his wife as Mr and Mrs Edwards out of respect, their Christian names were Frank and Elizabeth (Cissie). Mrs Edwards and I bonded immediately and she advised me on social events and leisure pastimes often accompanying me in the early days until I "knew the ropes".

I rarely went out during the week because I had to be up for work each morning at 5.30 am.

I found the lack of light inhibiting as far as my needlework hobbies were concerned. That first night, having completed the day's tasks I made myself a hot drink at 9 o'clock, lit one of the candles and climbed the stairs up to bed. Earlier I had managed to dip up water from the outhouse, hang it on the blackened hook, swing it over the fire (which had to be enlivened by means of a pair of bellows), boil it then carry it up to my bedroom and to the best of my ability have a strip down wash – there were no means whatsoever for bathing or showering but I made the best of a bad situation and always managed to keep up with my hygiene and cleanliness, difficult though it was. The room was spooky as I entered with my flickering candle, the light from which cast awesome moving shadows on the walls as I moved round the bed and placed it on the chair.

I threw back the covers of the bed and dropped, "plonk" on to the unrelenting straw mattress and there I sat taking stock of my position hitherto. No bath, no flush toilet, no wash basin, no electricity, no sink, no decent cooker, no radio, no car, no tractors and a bus that ran once a day on only two days each week and six miles from the nearest shop. It was like being on another planet. As I climbed into bed that night I could not help but shed a tear or two, I was so homesick and lonely. In fact I had a little weep every night for the next two weeks but then things seemed better. I guess that the disadvantages of the uncomfortable surroundings faded into the background as my relationship with the family developed. I had experienced quite a traumatic day, I was very, very tired and I eventually fell asleep to the patter of tiny feet running around my room – mice. My bedroom, I worked out, was situated above the house dairy where fruit and vegetables were stored, cheeses were made and racked and hams were cured and it was but a short journey up the dairy wall, through the bedroom floor and into my room. In time I even got used to their company.

Half past five on Tuesday came round far too quickly. I woke to the knocking on my bedroom door. "Right, I'm awake," I shouted then jumped out of bed, lit the candle and put on my working gear. Downstairs Mrs Edwards handed me a mug of what they called "sop". It was disgusting – tea poured over broken up pieces of bread then milk added. I really did try to eat it but when I encountered tea leaves floating in it, I gave up.

"I'll just have a cup of tea," I stated as I cut a slice of dry bread from the loaf. We couldn't linger over our snack as the milk lorry came each morning at half past eight. Hurriedly donning our boots in the outhouse we walked down the lane. I continued on to bring in the cows and our days work had begun. The milking procedure was carried on in the same way day in day out, and at nine o'clock we went in to a delicious cooked breakfast.

None of the cows had names and I quickly remedied that. Actually my first christening was that of the bull who in the future, to one and all, became William and woe betide anyone who referred to him as Bill or Billy – I always insisted on the use of his full, dignified name – William. Over the next few months I established a love/hate relationship with William. In a spare moment I would visit him in his stall, sit on the edge of the manger slightly to his right and smooth his huge hairy face. Invariably he would clumsily kneel on his fore legs then with a crash bordering on an earthquake he would drop en masse to the ground. From this position he would rest his head on my knees making it easier for me to scratch between his horns, beneath his jowls or simply continue to smooth down the whole of his face. The saliva would stream from his nostrils and mouth drenching my dungarees and I was always alert to the chance that he would suddenly shake his head. I was very aware of his dangerous horns.

After breakfast I would feed the pigs and any dry stock before turning my attention to William. I had to untether him and let him out into the farmyard for exercise and water. No matter how many times I performed this task I never felt confident in carrying it out. Always the adrenaline would start pumping and my heart thumping in my chest. The moment I released that t-bar through the ring and dropped his chain, I would turn and run "hell for leather" up the yard, into the barn and up the ladder to the top of the rick therein. It took William a little while to swing round his gigantic head but, as soon as he got out into the yard, he would charge after me up to the barn butting his head against the upright post to which the doors were secured. Mostly by this time his aggression had abated but on more than one occasion the upright post became dislodged from its slots, the barn doors would fly open allowing William into the barn. He would stand below me as I perched atop the hay rick but eventually he gave up the chase and quietly turned and lumbered out into the yard again. From habit he would always vent his frustration on the small garden gate, hooking his horns between the bars, unhitching the gate and tossing it up the garden. Fortunately he never attempted to go up into the garden probably judging that he was twice as wide as the opening. From here on in he settled down and took his fill of water then walked around the dungheap a few times, nosing shed doors and being inquisitive in general. Meantime, keeping a wary eye on him, I had to muck out his stall and replace his soiled bedding.

Well, now I had let him out without mishap but the part I dreaded most was getting him back in his stall and tying him up again. I felt vulnerable because I had to go into his byre ahead of him, creep through a small opening into the long cowshed and, through this opening place his hay, roots, oats and a few knobs of cattle cake into his manger. Everything prepared I rattled a bucket and called, "How up, William!" and in he would calmly trot with apparently nothing on his mind but food. Whilst he was thus engrossed I whipped around in with him, and he allowed me to hitch up the strong chain around his neck. He was only let out once a day but, as there were no drinking basins in the stalls, I would carry in a couple of buckets of water for him after letting the cows out each evening.

My exciting relationship with William only lasted three to four months because around Christmastime Mr Edwards purchased his replacement at Exeter Bull Sale thus bringing about the demise of William via Honiton cattle market. His successor I christened Ferdinand!

* * *

SCRUMPY

During the hours when my services were not required for the care of the herd and other livestock, I was given the task of preparing for cider making. Mr Edwards explained what needed doing and left me to get on with it. Firstly I had to clean the cider store, the press house and then the huge hogs heads (casks) and tubs required for the process. I was supplied with a bucket; cloths and a hard-bristled scrubbing brush for use on the solid oak press, the barrels and tubs (hogs head cut in half). The rooms had walls of bare stone which had been lime washed and everywhere hung curtains of cobwebs, I also had the use of a stiff yard brush and lipped shovel and lastly two goose wings. I assumed that the brush and shovel were for the purpose of cleaning the rough cobbled floors but what on earth did I use the goose wings for, I asked!

"They's better'n ought vor cleaning daun't cobwebs." I was informed and, quite frankly, they were. The tips poked into every nook and cranny and the stout wings made excellent brushes when scooping down the cobwebs. It took a long time and a lot of hard work before I was totally satisfied with the cleanliness of the houses. The low ceilings were made of bare wood and oaken cross beams and they were absolutely thick with webs. Spiders in profusion, of all shapes and sizes scuttled everywhere. Delving behind the barrels in the cider storeroom – barrels which were laid sideways and trigged into stable positions with wooden wedges – was quite difficult but I eventually surveyed the end results with pride. (Even the master remarked that they had never had such a thorough "going over".) Another task in the preparations was rinsing the interiors of the empty hogs heads with pure, unadulterated spring water. Taking out the bungs I poured this water into the barrels and when they were full, released it via the tap holes, ensuring a good flow of water infiltrated the casks which were then left to soak in the stream where I periodically turned them so that the wood swelled thus creating a tight seal of the cooper's slats.

Mr Edwards rebuilt one cask completely from the curved slats, circular top and base and steel bands and a very good job he made of it too.

After only a few days on the farm I already realised that nothing, but nothing was wasted. All metal was needed for the war effort so that the whole country was devoid of metal gates, railings, obsolete machinery etc. We salvaged used nails, hammering them into shape and soaking them in oil and binder twine (string) was meticulously unravelled and hung on spe-

cial hooks in the wagon house. Anything that could be salvaged was.
By Friday all was ready for the production of our Devonshire Cider and I was eager and interested to learn how it would be done. Another couple of weeks passed before we commenced.

A huge Devon cider press, complete with granite trough where the squeezed apple juice was collected.

To the Future

After milking and carrying out necessary yard work each Saturday I was given the half day off and, of course, I met up with Stoney – sometimes in Exeter, sometimes he would come to Honiton and on a couple of occasions we managed to revisit Whimple.

He always made sure I got back to the farm safely no matter what and it must have taken him half the night returning to his quarters. (I think these were somewhere in the Dartmouth area from a remark inadvertently made by Al on one occasion, but I was never sure).

We grew closer and closer and parting became almost unbearable. At one of our December rendezvous he said he had something important to discuss with me. Owing to the invasion of Europe the whole area was heaving with servicemen of every nationality and privacy was hard to come by. We managed to find a quiet corner in a very old inn. Stoney sat facing me and he took both my hands in his across the table.

"Micky, I know we haven't known each other long and that the world's gone crazy but I want you with me for ever so" (here he paused) "do you agree for me to have a word with the padre' about us tying the knot?" I was very young and so in love with this man and, in retrospect, I hadn't thought the implications through in depth.

"You mean right now? Immediately?" I said.

"I'll get an appointment as soon as I can."

"There's something else Stoney," I added, "I am only seventeen and need my parents' consent in writing, but I'll write home right away." (In 1944 you needed parental consent to marry until you reached twenty one).

And so that evening we parted full of love and hopes of a future together, whatever and wherever that would be.

The following day was Sunday, a day when only essential work was carried out on the farm which meant that I had the middle part of the day at leisure. As on every Sunday I cleaned my room whilst Sunday dinner was being prepared and then in the afternoon I wrote to my mother, who had sole custody of me, explaining what we planned and pleading with her to give us her blessing. Freddie Smith, the postman, took my letter for posting the following day.

CIDER MAKING

Having prepared everything required for cider making I told Mr Edwards that most of the stalls, sheds, sties and stables need a good cleaning and so tacked these tasks over the following ten days.

It was a Monday morning when the boss told me that he was off to visit neighbouring farms to solicit help for pressing the cider.

What a wonderfully helpful and friendly attitude there was between neighbours! Each and every farmer willing to help their peers whenever specific tasks required more labour than they had at hand.

"Ise never had zuch eager volunteers," he remarked on his return, "Having a Land Girl does have its advantages."

And so we started the interesting process of cider making …. An apple grinder (manually operated, of course) was strategically placed beneath a chute made for a hessian sack. This chute fed apples form the loft above into the body of the grinder. I was sent up the outside ladder leading to the loft and my instructions were to push the apples into the chute from above.

Meanwhile Mr Edwards tidily laid a base of good, clean straw on the cider press. Then Roy and I manually turned the huge handle of the grinder, which then spewed out the apple pulp into a large tub below. It was our responsibility to keep a good supply of pulp prepared for the master who was building the cider cheese. Turning the grinder handle was tough going. It was obvious that the cheese building was a specialised art – it had to be evenly spread over the oaken press base and kept to the correct size. Mr Edwards had been performing this task for as long as he could remember and he was obviously a master of the art.

On top of the straw base he shovelled the pulp, then straw and so on until the cheese was of the correct height and width. This accomplished, the square oak lid was gently screwed down into position over the cheese, just enough to place a gentle pressure on it. Before long the juice started to ooze out from the cheese base gently flowing into the huge collecting tub. It was then left overnight allowing the delicious juice to seep slowly out. We checked the apparatus periodically and when necessary, dipped up the juice from the tub and transferred it via a funnel into the large cider cask next door in the cider house. About ten thirty on the following day three of the neighbouring farmers arrived and the pressing of the cheese began in earnest. Roy wasn't at work that day so the four of us, with the use of a long, heavy, iron bar gently turned the huge screw on the lid of the press, squeezing out the liquid.

Mr Edwards stood by to observe. Apparently had the cheese been incorrectly constructed and off balance the sides could spew out causing great problems. On this occasion however all went according to plan. The cheese remained square and upright as the apple juice flowed out abundantly. Between short breaks we pushed the bar repeatedly, tightening the screw again and again. Finally the boss signalled that was enough so the farmers left. Consistently I transferred the juice to the cider house and was amazed at the amount which had oozed out. Again the cheese was left to stand overnight until the flow slowed to a mere drip and finally stopped.

We left the bungs out of the casks and they were not replaced until complete fermentation had taken place and all the impurities in the form of a gassy froth exuded. Once this eased off the bungs were hammered back into place.

As I said, nothing ever went to waste and so the dried-out remains of the cheese were fed in rationed amounts to the cows.

On the morning following the completion of our cider making, I crossed the lane and opened the press house in order to transfer the last of the juice. I flung open the door and was amazed to see a hen stagger out, head to one side and wings so relaxed that the tips scraped the ground – obviously a very inebriated chicken. She must have got into the press house the previous evening and had been unwittingly shut in. She must have helped herself to the new cider, deliciously sweet, and was very, very drunk.

All visitors to the farm were invited to sample our home produced cider. Every day the postman, Freddie Smith, who delivered out mail on horseback, frequented the cider store to "quench his thirst". Now this invitation had probably been extended to him by most of the other farmers on his post round and as we were one of his last calls, he was invariably quite sozzled by the time he reached us. I recall on one certain morning he arrived wet through. His post bag was soaked, water still dripping out and his uniform was very wet. He handed the post bag to me.

"Maid, do I a favour," he said, "I fell off of me 'orse into t'river at Charleshayes Ford. Do ee try and dry me letters," he asked.

I took the saturated bag and rummaged inside, extricating a small bundle of letters etc. The addresses on this wet mail were absolutely illegibly blurred and there was no way I would be able to get them dry in time for him to delivery.

"Sorry Freddie, no can do," I remarked as I handed the postbag and its contents back to him. I never learned how he got out of that predicament. However, he turned up next day and every day thereafter – always "three sheets to the wind" from his cider capers. When I first became acquainted with him he had no home but slept in a chicken shed in a field across the valley from Kitts Farm. Most of his life was spent in the Sidmouth Arms during opening hours. He was fairly old and had never married. But Freddie's luck was in. Lord and Lady Sidmouth owned the large manor in Upottery village. This manor, now demolished, was set in beautiful parklands. Shortly after the commencement of hostilities they moved their staff from their London home and took up permanent residence in the Manor presumably to avoid the London blitz.

Now her ladyship had a middle-aged, petite cockney lady-in-waiting named Winnie and it wasn't long before Freddie set his cap at her. Both were single, both loved a tipple and soon Freddie was doing some serious courting eventually proposing to Winnie. She accepted and they were allowed to move into the Manor Lodge, a lovely little cottage just within the gates to the Manor, as a "grace and favour" home. They made a lovely little couple (both were small in stature) and Winnie took good care of her Freddie. They lived there happily with each other until death parted them.

THWARTED LOVE

Being so very busy, the days passed quickly by and my mother wasted no time in answering my letter in which I had asked her to agree to my marriage. I eagerly opened the letter with hopeful anticipation yet not a little apprehension. Disappointment mingled with anger as I read the brief note, which flatly and conclusively refused consent to any proposed union. Of course, older an wiser, I look back and realise how justified she was in her decision but at that moment in time I felt my eyes fill up with hot tears and the feeling of despair was combined with a sense of anger and frustration. As fate decreed it was of little consequence because at our next meeting Stoney informed me that his commanding officer was totally in disagreement also. His padre had apparently been more sympathetic but totally in agreement with the C.O.'s views. "Times were so uncertain and with the recent invasion of the continent Stoney's embarkation could well be imminent," he was told. "Wait until hostilities cease."

Form the heights of our expectations when we had previously met and made plans we now plunged into the depths of despair. We were both so very depressed at the outcome and, on parting, I quietly sobbed as I walked the last few yards to the farmhouse after leaving Stoney that night.

APPROACH OF WINTER

And so I fell into the daily routine once more. As all harvesting had been completed our mid-day tasks revolved around farm maintenance. There were always five barred gates to be repaired, gate posts to be replaced, partitions between stalls to be renewed as well as the odd shed to be lime-washed. (This was a job I did not relish as just a tiny splash of lime on the skin left it red and sore and, as we had no goggles, great care was needed in applying the wash to avoid contact with the eyes).

Day by day my own particular sphere of the farmwork, centred around the cowsheds and courtyard, improved, for I took great pride in bringing it all up to my standards of cleanliness. The cowsheds were cobbled with just a gutter which had been concreted. This gutter ran the full length of the shed and carried away water and liquid affluent. The courtyard also was cobbled with quite a steep gradient and cleaning it took a lot of time and hard work, getting the stiff bristles of the yard brush in and around the cracks. It was made more difficult because of the huge dung heap from which liquid manure oozed. This was a constant flow to the lowest level of the yard and then out through an underground drain. That dung heap really had to go I decided, but it was another year before I got my wish. I cleaned out sheds and stalls, some of which were a foot deep in muck and soiled straw bedding. It took me ages to become accustomed to the occasional rat, which would scuttle out from hay and straw and from behind sacks of stored corn. An extra cheeky one would sit near me washing behind its ears via its saliva moistened paws whilst I was milking.

The days became shorter and darkness fell much earlier necessitating the use of storm lanterns and strategically placed candles in the cow sheds for milking times.

I have always loved to sing and Mr Edwards vowed that after my arrival the milk yield was greater due to my serenading the cows whilst milking. He himself, however, did not always appreciate my repertoire. Occasionally I would belt out "Jerusalem", "The Holy City" or aria from the "Desert Song" but mainly my choice would be the pop of the day.

I recall that one song ended with " .... Oh when will I see him again? Quack! Quack! Mmmm Quack, Quack! When will I see him again?" no matter where he was and if he heard me singing this song, he would loudly shout, "'Nough o' thick 'ole lore!" (Translated "Enough of that old rubbish") and then he would guffaw heartily.

One day, having completed the task in hand, I went indoors to ask Mrs Edwards if she knew where the boss was.

"Up top linney," she said.

So I trudged my way up the lane in the direction of the top linney. As I approached the gateway entrance I heard the melodic sounds of, "Mares ee dotes and does ee dotes and liddle lambs ee ivy, a kid'll ee divy too wouldn't you."

Leaning over the gate I shouted as loudly as I could: "'Nough o' thick 'ole lore!"

He had unwittingly picked up the words and tune of the silly song I used to sing and had burst forth with this nonsense song (popular at the time) without even thinking what he was singing. I teased him about this incident in the following weeks.

Approximately two weeks before Christmas, as we were sitting down to Sunday lunch Mr Edwards turned to me "Thees know, maid, thees worked danged hard vor I these past weeks so if thees minded to go home vor Christmas I'll give ee a week off. Can't pay 'ee mind but thees welcome to a week off." I was over the moon as I had been quite homesick intermittently. In fact I cried myself to sleep most nights for the first two weeks or so – I felt so lonely, hundreds of miles form home, and so isolated.

I had a great time with Stoney in Exeter prior to my leave. I asked him to come home with me but he said that leave for him at that time was out of the question but he suggested it might be a good opportunity to win my mother over. Once again parting and seeing him walk away up Kitts Lane was so hard but we had arranged our next tryst in the New Year.

The next couple of weeks were very busy for Mrs Edwards and Gladys. All the Christmas poultry had to be killed, plucked and drawn – geese, chickens and ducks – and there was a perpetual smell of burnt feathers as the final down was singed. Thankfully I was not asked to be involved in any of these tasks.

First Leave

As I cleaned and pressed (with an old flat iron) my dress uniform it suddenly dawned on me that I was going to see my mum and sisters again. I was so excited to be going home for Christmas.

Quite unexpectedly, as I was almost ready to leave to catch the bus to Taunton, Mr Edwards presented me with two large parcels.

"Tech these eer, maid, an 'ave a Happy Christmas and doan 'ee vorget to come back."

He and his wife had, in fact, packed a lovely, large goose in one parcel and Bramley and Russet apples in another. What a lovely gesture and one which my mother truly appreciated when I eventually arrived home!

My train to Manchester left Taunton at midnight and as my one and only bus left Upottery in the morning, it meant I had to while away the day in town. It seemed to be a long, endless day. I treated myself to dinner in Deller's Restaurant (now a night club) across the bridge over the River Tone, did some window shopping before going to the matinee at the cinema which was unexpectedly full with service men and women. Part way through the film a Yankee soldier who happened to be sitting alongside me craftily and suggestively put his hand on my thigh. I quickly changed seats. I must admit wearing jodhpurs had great advantages in such situations. The film show ended so I exited the cinema and made my way to the station and spent the next few hours in the Church Army Canteen, which was facing the rear entrance. Time dragged by and I was so relieved when midnight approached and I was able to start my journey home in earnest. In all truthfulness once I was able to rest and relax I was overcome by a kind of weariness during the first couple of days when I arrived home at Rishton in Lancashire. I really had worked very hard over the past four months, rising at 5 am or 5.30 am and working throughout the day until 8 pm and later at night with very little respite. I simply wanted to rest and take things easy with my family over the Christmas period. My mother would not change her mind regarding my marriage and I respected her decision. The week passed all too quickly. All too soon I was on the train travelling southwards towards Devon.

My new found family at Upottery welcomed me back with open arms seemingly relieved at my return and, frankly, I was pleased to get back into my routine with my beloved cows, pigs, horses and Watch and Towser the cattle dogs. There was one other animal of whom I had become very fond and that was a spaniel gun-dog called Sport. He was the masters' pride and joy, apparently being an excellent retriever of game. Unlike Watch and Towser who were never allowed inside the farmhouse, Sport had his own tatty but comfortable easy chair in a corner of the living room. He only went outdoors on shooting expeditions and in the evenings when all daily tasks had been completed. It was then that Mr Edwards, gun tucked under his arm, would walk around his acres of farmland checking that all the sheep were present and problem free and that the horses were grazing where they should be. He was always escorted by Sport. He explained to me how on once occasion whilst doing his evening round, he was sure he saw the form of a white parachute dangling from the lower branches of a tree. Such was his concern that he cocked his gun and took aim as he slowly approached the offending white patch in the semi-darkness only to discover as he got nearer that it was the white triangular shaped patch on Frolic's face. After that we used to tease him about the time he almost shot his own horse!

Sport, on the whole, was a very well disciplined dog but, on a rare occasion when the backhouse door had been inadvertently left off the latch, he would escape. Mr Edwards would become frantic, walking the fields, calling and whistling but all to no avail for Sport always returned in his own good time. He was then in disgrace for several days.

Since arriving at Kitts in September I had occasionally put in an appearance at the weekly whist drive which took place every Tuesday evening in The Manor Room. The Manor Room was the village hall and the centre of the local social activities etc. Whist drives, dances, concerts, meetings of the WI and MU, harvest home feasts etc. The Justice Room, however, was situated alongside the Manor Stables and it was here where Lord Sidmouth's tenants paid their rents on Lady Day and at Michaelmas, where farmers met with his Lordship to discuss any problems they encountered, where disputes were settled and even where on the rare occasions tenants were summoned to sort out domestic problems. (Hence the Justice Room).

I had played whist at home with friends and family and I quickly picked up the rules of progressive whist. I really enjoyed these evenings and soon became quite adept, winning on many occasions and learning how not to provoke the wrath of my partners by playing with thought, and therefore causing no offence. Some players took these sessions very, very seriously. Half way through we would take a break for the inevitable Devon Splits (small buns with preserve and clotted cream) and tea, and then I would be approached by young farmers with offers to escort me home but being besotted with Stoney, I politely turned them down.

My work took up all the daylight hours during that week and I looked forward to meeting up with my handsome US sailor again. That Saturday I set out excitedly, arriving at the entrance to Central Station in Exeter where we had arranged to meet – but there was no sign of Stoney. I waited, I waited and I waited to no avail – there was no sign of Stoney. Eventually I strolled along to The Allied Services Club and scanned the faces there only to met with utter disappointment. I was gutted! It became clear that he was not going to put in an appearance so I melancholically made the journey back to Honiton and thence to the farm – dejected, depressed but mainly very concerned for his well-being.

All I could do now was to patiently wait in the hope that he would contact me.

Winter

Iploughed all my energies into my work over the following weeks. More hours were needed in the management of the herd. Bad weather meant that the cows remained in their stalls and this, in turn, called for more mucking out and feeding round. There were no individual drinking basins as there had been at Whimple House Farm and this necessitated all the stock being turned out into the courtyard for water and exercise. They took it in turns to drink from the "chattrelle" and meandered around the dung heap whilst I took the advantage to clean down the byres. Mangolds and swede's had to be ground and this was extremely hard work continually turning the wheel of the grinder manually. Come rain or shine kale had to be cut and hauled and this I did unaided. In dry weather it was quite a pleasant task all be it physically demanding but when it rained I would end up soaked to the skin. I found it too difficult to manoeuvre whilst wearing oil skins, my mac was not supple, making each stroke with the wood hook hard work and I therefore tackled this task wearing my green sweater over my working garb. On very cold days my hands felt as though they were frozen to the kale stems.

I quickly learned how to harness up and handle the huge shire horses gradually building up my confidence until I finally had a fantastic rapport with them. Equally they just seemed to accept me and invariably co-operated whole-heartedly in carrying out whatever I asked of them. By their individual natures they each had their little foibles with which I was able to deal and admittedly I was wary of Bob – she was liable to lash out with her left hind leg without reason or warning but in the main they all worked very hard, seemingly to anticipate what was expected of them.

All this additional work during the Winter months in and around the farmyard meant that there was little time left for much field work. Ditching had to be done. This meant clearing the channel where the water ran downhill alongside the hedges and heaping the offending debris on top of the hedges. Picking up stones was another job to be done. We had two four-acre fields about a mile from the farm along the A30 in the Taunton direction. (These fields were quite separate form the rest of our ground). I would harness up Frolic and set off in the putt, which carried a sack, a bucket, a bottle of cider and a hunk of bread and cheese making my way up to these fields.

◎§§~

Left: *Mr Edwards with Sport.*

Above: *Pansy, Gladys, and Mr Edwards with Sport.*

Above: *Pansy and Mr Edwards.*

◎§§~

Right: *Mrs Edwards with her pullets and Towser*

Starting at a corner I would mark out a square on the bare ground roughly six yards across using four large stones as markers. Then I would clear this
area heaping the stones in the centre of the square. This portion cleared, I
marked off the next square and continued in this fashion clearing the field
square by square. This ground on top of the hill proved to be very stoney
and although my fingers were very sore to start with they soon became
toughened up and my nails were certainly well filed. I carried an old pocket watch so at one o'clock I would sit on the sack and, leaning against the
hedgerow, eat my 'elegant' meal – bread, cheese and cider and rest my
aching back. At some future date Roy or Mr Edwards would bring up the
wagon and a large fork with closely set bent prongs especially suitable for
loading the stones. These were then tipped out and spread along the rough
track leading from the main road to our fields. The last load of the day
would be carted home to the farm to pave around the wood pile and the
hayshed firming up the soft ground. My days spent up the top of the hill
were quite lonely but at 3.30 pm I would pile everything onto the putt and
set off home in time to attend to the cows before going in to tea. This was
not the end of the day because milking was always carried out after tea. My
home bound journey was always interrupted by Bert who managed his
father's farm, Crinhayes, off the A30. He would always pop out and pass
the time of day with me on my journey usually making derogatory remarks
about the absent-sided putt. Bert was quite a character.

COUNTRY SPORT

After Christmas the farmers organised their rabbiting parties. In turn they
would arrange an all day shoot at their respective farms and this culminated with an extravagant party in the evening. Invited members of the
shooting party dined with their host at midday and their families would
join them in the evening for a wonderful supper. The women folk pulled
out all the stops on these occasions working extremely hard, baking and
cooking for days prior to the shoot and this culminated in a marvellous
spread of food. Cider, of course, would flow freely so that everybody
relaxed. The atmosphere was convivial and after supper the men folk
played cards whilst the women engaged in conversation (gossiped) around
a roaring log fire. I was invariably invited to these events along with Gladys
and Mrs Edwards but most times I turned up late as I had to do all the milking by myself on these occasions, and to milk the whole herd single handed was time consuming. Often I would turn up so tired that, relaxing in a
comfortable chair by a blazing fire, I would quickly fall asleep. (Once whilst
I was asleep the men folk tied my shoe laces together and they were highly amused when I unwittingly tried to walk and went sprawling) I would
like to explain that on these tenant farmer's "shoots" rabbits were the only

quarry because they were forbidden by their landlord, Viscount Sidmouth, to poach his pheasants. These birds were especially hatched and reared by his lordship's gamekeeper and when in season they were released at "shooting parties" for the sport of Lord Sidmouth, his friends and even some members of the aristocracy. Farm labourers were hired as beaters for as long as these shooting parties lasted and they could last for several days. Although it was strictly forbidden for anyone else to shoot a pheasant, one mysteriously turned up discreetly on our dinner table from time to time!!

A NEW YEAR – A NEW BULL

William had become increasingly more difficult to handle – he really was a "grumpy old man" and unfortunately for him the master considered he was past his best as a working bull, in fact his days were numbered. In the early part of the New Year a large Bull Sale was to be held at Exeter and shortly before this took place poor William was sold for beef at Honiton market.

On the day of the sale Mr Edwards was collected by Mr Fone, the cattle haulier and they set out determined to purchase William's replacement. Now Mr Fone had a reputation for being partial, no very partial, to a drink or two, or three or ....., so when they had not arrived home by the time we had finished up the day's chores, Mrs Edwards began to look very concerned.

It was quite late and very dark when the lorry rolled up to the gates of the courtyard and the human occupants were 'worse for drink'. In fact to this day I don't know how Mr Fone had managed to drive the lorry back at all, he was in such a state. Mrs Edwards and I held up lighted storm lanterns and watched the fiasco of two inebriated men trying to unload a frisky young bull and pen and tether him. It could have been disastrous but it was so funny and apparently it was the norm for this particular haulier. It was the one and only time I ever saw Mr Edwards worse for drink in my life.

On the following morning, when yard duties had been completed, we decided to let the young bull out together being that his temperament was an unknown quantity! I had already decided that his name was to be Ferdinand. He was, of course, not so huge as William although of the same Devon Red breed. He also seemed to be somewhat milder mannered, quite young, and frisky at times, but without the malevolence to which I had been accustomed from William. Mr Edwards said he was sixteen months old. When he was untethered he simply wandered around the yard, too inquisitive to be bothered with we humans. The boss tied a double length of binder twine through his nose ring and invited me to walk him around. Ferdinand accepted this method of exercising extremely well. On a few occasions he would all of a sudden jump around flinging his hind legs one way and then the other making it difficult for me to keep up with him but he seemed more playful than nasty and a short, sharp tug on the string attached to his ring brought him down to earth. Yes, I considered that this was a big improvement after my daily dread of dealing with William.

Early that spring I suggested to the boss that we ought to clean out the Higher Linney. This consisted of open stalls with a roof for shelter. There were feeding mangers as well as a stream-fed water trough and here dry stock such as in-calf heifers, yearlings, steers, fat stock, maiden heifers had Winter quarters. There was a large paddock and the bullocks could roam around freely. A small hayshed situated at the rear of the linney facilitated feeding and the whole of the linney was only about one hundred and fifty yards up the lane which enabled us to keep check on whatever stock was there.

I had noticed that the paddock badly needed cleaning. The water did not appear to drain away easily and I considered that the dung heap blocked the flow of any liquid. There was always a kind of seepage of liquid manure around the dung heap, which was gradually spreading outwards. After we had carted out the dung and swept the cobbles clean it looked totally different. It quickly dried out, seemed more spacious and far more comfortable for the bullocks. I managed to spread the adjoining field with the dung over the following days.

During my working life at Kitts Farm, Mr Edwards encouraged me to work with the horses. He said that I had a natural aptitude and so I was allowed to carry out all tasks involving the horses with the exception of two. I was not allowed to attempt ploughing. The boss maintained that such strain could ruin a woman and, despite my pleas to attempt it, he was quite adamant. He flatly refused. As did he when haymaking time approached. He would not agree to teach me how to use the mowing machine.

"Much too dangerous," he persisted.

And so he started ploughing ready for Spring sowing whilst I was allowed to use the Shire horses for rolling and dragging, often working a team of two at once. But he always ploughed. I also spent many days preparing the meadowland for cutting later on in the haymaking season. This entailed slashing out docks and dashels (thistles) before rolling the ground using a horse-drawn roller. I must have walked hundreds of miles, back and forth, leading the horse across the fields, flattening the uneven ground and giving the fields a tailored look, the grass forming shining stripes.

VILLAGE SOCIAL LIFE

The weeks passed quickly by – one, two, three and still no news of Stoney. I could see no purpose in travelling to Exeter and I began to join in with the local social events greatly encouraged by Mrs Edwards. In addition to

American Servicemen frequently attending local dances. Bases at Upottery (USAAF) and Dunkeswell (USN) brought thousands of airmen and groundcrew to this remote part of Devon.

the Tuesday evening Whist Drives in the Manor Room, there was no shortage of village dances both at Upottery and in the surrounding villages. Mrs Edwards accompanied me to the first dance I attended in the Manor Room. Preparing for this dance I strip washed, donned my bright red dress and red clog-type sandals and took extra special care with my make-up. Finally I tucked an artificial red rose behind my ear as I had been wont to do when I danced at Tony's Ballroom in Blackburn. What a shock I got on entering the village hall! The men and boys wore suits, neat shirts with ties and the girls and women were in grey, navy or brown skirts with white, buttoned to the throat blouses, long-sleeved, of course.

I felt like a "lady of the night – the lady in red" – the only one in step! I was, however, very popular with the gentlemen, and consequently very unpopular with the farmers' daughters. But it wasn't long before fashions for these ladies livened up somewhat at future dances and festivities and I like to think that maybe, just maybe, I had started a precedent for fashion in the "sticks".

The music at these hops was always supplied by local bands, usually accordion bands consisting of two piano accordionists, a pianist and a drummer or percussionist. Eddie Selway and His Accordion Band and the Matthews family proved to be extremely popular. Around this era Jimmy Shand, the famous Scot accordionist was really popular and the local musicians tried to emulate his style particularly when country dances were included in the programme, and very well they did it. Nobody danced the jive or jitterbug at these local dances but whenever the Yanks promoted a dance at their bases which abounded in this area, the halls heaved and bounced from the beat of their Big Band music and the resulting be-bopping. Their bands were huge and very professional and they played tunes made famous by Glen Miller, Jimmy Dorsey etc. I often accepted the invitation to their dances at Dunkeswell and they would arrange to collect me by Jeep and ensure I was returned to the farm safely. Those dances really were fun, full of laughter and vitality but usually I paid the penalty the following day when I still had to be up by five to start work feeling completely exhausted.

Having made one faux pas when attending that first dance I was about to make a second one, an occasion when I got it wrong yet again. I had the temerity to enter the Sidmouth Arms the village pub!

Where I had lived in the North of England a visit to the local pub, particularly at weekends, was the norm for most women but here apparently it was taboo. I must admit I was quite embarrassed on walking in to find that I was the only female present but the farmers' treated me with great respect and despite my absolute inaptitude they included me in their teams when playing table skittles or darts. The only light we had in the bar came from an old oil lamp, which was positioned just a little too close to the dart board for my comfort. I only drank soft drinks or an occasional shandy. Again it was not too long before the female population started to frequent The Sidmouth Arms.

NEIGHBOURS
Approximately five hundred yards along the lane in the direction of the village there was a small holding called "Down Elms". Here a lovely couple called Ed and Bessie Symes lived with their children, two daughters and three sons. The oldest son was none other than Eddie Selway of accordion band fame but Eddie was married with a family and his daytime employment was that of farm labourer for a farmer whose farm was on the opposite side of the valley. He lived in a "tied" cottage; I always considered the "tied cottage" system to be cruel and feudal. Briefly the cottage was one of the perks of the job, just as long as you remained in your bosses employ, but if for some reason, employment ceased, the worker had to relinquish the occupation of his home often with just a week's notice. This meant that a harsh and unscrupulous employer could make unreasonable demands of his employee who succumbed because he worked and lived with the fear of his family being evicted. I was aware of many such instances where this had occurred and bearing in mind that there was no comeback for unfair dismissal as there is nowadays, farm workers were very often held over the barrel of a gun, so to speak.

Eddie was one of the lucky ones, in that he had a fair employer in Mr Parrish and I believe he remained in his service until he retired. He and his band became increasingly popular so may be he took early retirement from his day job because he eventually bought a lovely detached bungalow.

Bessie Symes was a robust, red-cheeked, jolly lady and I loved her. She always welcomed me in her home and I appreciated this so much. Her children were all about my age – some a little younger, some a little older – one exactly my age and so we had a lot in common and we had such fun together. With such a large family Bessie worked extremely hard. Consider that she had no modern conveniences and washing, cleaning and cooking under those conditions for such a large family must have been very difficult and extremely tiring. Yet she always had a smile and a kind word and I never heard her complain. Ed and the boys were away on their respective jobs during the day, the youngest girl was still at school and the remaining daughter was in service on a neighbouring farm which meant that Bessie also did more than her share when their cows had to be attended to during the day. Despite working so hard she was always prepared to join us when, as a group, we cycled to Whist Drives or dances in neighbouring villages.

There would be about a dozen of us who would arrange a meeting place before setting out for Yarcombe, Luppitt, Churchinford, Smeatharp or even Honiton. What a happy, carefree crowd we were! It did not take me long to realise that a bicycle was essential in this isolated setting and the first time my liaison officer visited me I requested a Land Army cycle. She examined my bedroom and the living quarters and suggested to Mr and Mrs Edwards that a little more comfort would be appropriate, to no avail. The bicycle, however, arrived quite quickly. It was a hard bike to ride – Mr Edwards tried it out and commented that it was the only bike he had ever ridden where you had to pedal vigorously going down hill, but it got me from A to B making a difference to my social life.

Bessie always did the washing every alternate Monday at Kitts Farm and for this she was paid two shillings and sixpence (twelve and a half pence). A fire had to be lit beneath a copper boiler which Mr Edwards always filled the day before she came and when the water was hot enough it was transferred, as and when needed, to a huge zinc bath. Here she would spend all day rubbing the clothes by hand using a block of hard soap, rinsing and hanging out the washing up in the hay shed orchard. It was always spotlessly clean.

Directly above Down Elms was a cottage called Little Common, where dwelt old Jess Hunt and his wife. Jess had retired from farm work but was reputedly a master prize-winner when it came to laying a hedge. This was an art in itself and I was fortunate, at a later date, to have him as my tutor. Jess now did odd jobs at his own discretion and was often over at Kitts during haymaking and harvesting.

A further two hundred yards up the lane from Down Elms was the entrance to Preston Farm. This farm was owned by the mother of Mrs Edwards. She had the reputation of being a hard taskmaster, although her son, Art, managed the farm whilst two other brothers did the labouring and a younger daughter helped with the household chores. The old lady had worked extremely hard herself when her husband died prematurely leaving her with a large farm to run and five children to rear.

Just a short distance from the entrance to Preston Farm was another house which was called Kingston Cottage. This was occupied by a strange family. The husband and wife, Mr and Mrs Hardiman, her daughter from a previous marriage and a young school boy son. Mr and Mrs Edwards warned me never to accept any invitation to go there as it was a "house of ill repute", I later found out what they meant.

*   *   *

Each Sunday, after carrying out the essential jobs, I would give my bedroom a good clean whilst Sunday dinner was being cooked. On fine days I would take a stroll with Watch and Towser down by the River Otter before, once again, tackling the evening's milking etc. Only essential work was undertaken on Sunday. Mr Edwards' late father and then his older brother, Harry, were part-time lay preachers so obviously the boss himself had been reared with a very strict religious background. Nobody was allowed to sew, knit or partake in anything laborious on the Sabbath Day. Therefore being an avid needle woman, I would secretly sit up in my bedroom with my knitting or embroidery, nervously listening for the sound of a footstep on the landing and hurriedly pushing the offending article beneath the bedclothes if I heard the slightest sound of movement. I really felt guilty and dreaded being caught out.

There was a wireless in the living room which due to the lack of electricity was powered by wet accumulators. These batteries would run out and then we had to take them to Honiton to be recharged. They were heavy and cumbersome and had to be carried in an upright position. Remember we had to transport them by bus. Because of the hassle entailed we were not allowed to switch on this wireless except at nine in the morning, one in the afternoon, and nine in the evening just to hear the news and weather forecast.

If I decided I would like to attend the evening service at St Mary the Virgin's Church in Upottery village, we would commence milking earlier to enable me to wash, change and ride the two miles down to the village. I was never refused this request to attend Church although I didn't go on a regular basis.

One Saturday in early Spring I decided to travel to Exeter to look up some of my old Women's Land Army mates and I ended up in the same old corner of the Club, chatting away, when Alma walked in on the arm of a new beau.

"What happened to Al?" I discreetly enquired of her.

"We were going strong," she quipped, "but the last date we arranged he stood me up and I haven't seen hide nor hair of him since."

I explained that the same thing had happened to me with Stoney and we both agreed it was very peculiar.

She invited me to accompany her and her current boyfriend to the cinema but I excused myself saying, "Three's a crowd," and in any case I had to catch an early train back to Honiton if I were to connect up with the bus to Upottery.

That was the last time I saw Alma. We just lost touch but at a later date, much later, I heard through the grapevine that she had married a Norwegian sailor.

I meandered slowly back to the station and waited for my train when suddenly somebody caught hold of my arm. I whipped round sure that it was Stoney but it was a sergeant to whom Stoney had once introduced me.

"Can you spare a minute?" he said

"Just until my train arrives," I replied as he guided me into the waiting room

"This is so awkward," he said, "I daren't say too much, but I thought you should know – Stoney isn't coming back any more.

"Why?" I queried, taken aback.

He looked me straight in the eyes and said, "Stoney won't be going anywhere anymore.

"He's been killed, hasn't he?" I rejoined.

He didn't make any reply to my question but continued, "You're very young. You've got the future to look to so don't look back."

With this my train pulled up at the platform and this kind man hurriedly escorted me on to the train, clasped my hand, turned and walked away.

What interpretation could I put on that brief conversation? It left me in limbo, but in my heart I was sure he had been killed.

I mourned him, I still do mourn him but the sergeant was right. This was war. I was young with an important job to do and I just had to get on with life.

I tried hard to draw the curtain on my wonderful love affair but God, it hurt so much.

Springtime

One day in March Mrs Edwards passed on the latest news to me just as we were about to start dinner. Freddie Smith had told her that Fred Bartlett at Wellsprings Farm had a Land Girl. It was great news for me. I had made many acquaintances and a few really good friends since arriving in Upottery but I still felt I was the odd one out, a "vorriner". Mrs Edwards had been a good friend and mentor but I regarded her as a substitute mother; she was of an older generation. Mr Edwards had been my protector and surrogate father. He had put the crude, married milk lorryman in his place when he made a suggestive pass at me, and rescued me, by excusing my presence, when the lads who were helping with our threshing threw five mice at me aiming for my cleavage (how scary was that!?!) and he had shown me great respect from the very first day I started in his employ.

Gladys was my 'young sister' who had her own interests. It would be wonderful to have a friend of my own age not to mention somebody in the same situation. Imagine my surprise and joy when I discovered that the newly arrived Land Girl was none other than Kathy, the girl I first met at the Women's Land Army interview at Blackburn and later when we trained together at Whimple. Henceforth we attended local socials, dances, etc. together. She had been sent to a farm near Torrington on leaving Whimple House and her billet had been dreadful – the bedroom windows did not even have any glass in them and she had had to prop her suitcase in the opening for protection from the elements. That Winter had been a hard one, cold, wet and snowy. She was so cold at night that she slept partly dressed, piling her greatcoat and even the mat from the floor on top of her.

Apparently there had been nine Land Girls assigned to this farm over the period of the previous twelve months, all unable to withstand the isolated and harsh conditions.

As in my case, Kathy had received a good education (in a Convent), had left a good clerical job and had lived in a nice four-bedroomed house in Lancashire with every modern comfort. We knew that being in the Land Army was going to be tough and sacrifices had to be made, but two things were essential when taking on this job. Firstly good nourishing food and secondly a good night's sleep.

Kathy persevered with the conditions for six long, cold winter months. Unable to cope with the extreme discomfort any longer she had applied for a transfer and now here she was at Upottery and in comparative luxury. She even had sheepskin rugs in her room at Wellsprings Farm. Mr and Mrs Bartlett and their two young sons welcomed her as one of the family. She was married in 1948 and remains in touch with them weekly.

PRISONERS-OF-WAR

At the end of February Mr Edwards announced that he had earlier accepted the offer of two German Prisoners-of-War for labouring on the farm. Freddie had just delivered his notification and they were to start work the following day. It really came as a shock to me as I had no prior warning or intimation of this decision. I realised that Roy did not now put in regular attendances of late owing to illness and family problems but German Prisoners-of-War was the last solution I would have thought of. Sad thoughts passed through my mind of the people and friends I had met and lost due to this war, not the least being Stoney, and at that moment in time I was in no way feeling well disposed to the Germans – now I was expected to work alongside them.

"There's instructions here, maid, that they're to do their work and we haven't to feed them or socialise with them in any way, shape or form," declared the boss.

"Fraternisation? You must be joking," I thought.

As we expected the Army lorry arrived at about ten o'clock and two young men, jumped from the back. One was fair, short and thick set and the other was the complete opposite – tall, dark and slim in stature. They each carried a packet, presumably their lunch and what appeared to be a rolled up cape. Neither could speak English so with the odd word and an accompanying gesture, Mr Edwards directed them to follow me.

That morning's task was to cut up a recently felled tree into manageable lengths then haul it up to the wood pile in the hayshed orchard which was situated behind the farmhouse. I marked off a sample length by notching the tree with a saw and miming the motions of sawing, left them with a hand saw and a crosscut saw to complete the job. They worked reasonably well and when at one o'clock Mr Edwards brought out a jug of tea and mugs they unwrapped their lunch packets and dined off a thick wedge of dry bread and a small portion of dry, crusty cheese. After lunch I harnessed up Frolic and we loaded up the logs, hauling them to the woodpile. Their lorry returned to collect them around four in the afternoon. And so the days passed on.

We learnt that the fair man was called Koed Ullricht and the dark one was Paul Weissz. It was obvious from his somewhat reluctant attitude that Koed resented working for us. His work was slow and untidy and he dragged out the chores unnecessarily. I thought he was a bit scary. In all fairness, maybe farm work was new to Koed and not to his liking. After all it was mainly hard physical toil. Paul, however, seemed pleased to have something to occupy his time and he co-operated well even trying to pick up the odd English word.

They had been with us for a couple of weeks when Mr Edwards told me to cut and haul in a couple of good loads of kale from Roundabout. The field had to be cleared and prepared for ploughing as he intended to sow the entire field with mangold. "Tek the Jerry's with 'ee, maid. Let them cut and load. See to Bob and keep an eye on things," were his instructions. Perhaps it was rather silly but I did feel somewhat concerned as I grabbed two wood hooks, put Bob between the shafts of the wagon and indicated that they follow me. The day was fine but the kale tops still dripped from the previous night's rain and I beckoned them to watch me as I grasped the thick kale stalk and made one clean thrust with the wood hook, at an angle, through its base. After cutting a couple more stalks I handed a hook to each man and pointed to the kale. They carried on cutting the stems but threw them back higgledy-piggledy, so, between moving Bob on, I stacked the kale in neat piles to facilitate its loading. The morning passed on uneventfully when suddenly a piercing scream rent the air. I turned round to see Koed with a limp, hanging hand, dripping with blood. There was a terrible gash across the full width of the back of his hand where he had slashed it with the wood hook and thick, globules of adipose tissue oozed out along with the blood. I tried to put and hold the flesh edges together whilst Paul bound the wound tightly with his and Koed's handkerchiefs and together we managed to get him on the wagon. Paul supported him whilst I drove in haste back to the farmhouse. Here we left Koed in the care of Mr and Mrs Edwards then returned to resume our job. That was the last we saw of Koed and I never learned how bad his injury turned out to be, but at the back of my mind lurked the morbid thought that it could have been an intentionally inflicted action which perhaps resulted in a more serious injury than had been intended. Koed had seemed to be averse to working for us from the start. He had been a reluctant worker and I wondered (and may be I was wrong) if this was his way of jacking in. Following this trauma Paul turned up alone in the future and guess who was the first to break the non-fraternisation? Why! The boss of course! When I challenged him about his invitation to Paul to partake of our dinner each day in the farmhouse his excuse was, "Well we've virtually won the war and anyway how can they expect to get a good day's work out of a fella on the rations they hand out?"

Henceforth Paul sat down to a good meal every day. The boss had fixed up a dartboard on the stair partition and after dinner we all played darts for half an hour or so. One thing I remember about Paul on these occasions was that he hated to lose, especially to me, a woman. Otherwise he was the perfect gentleman in every way. Gradually he picked up a few words and phrases of English, which helped with communication. He would always open the gates allowing me to pass through before him and many times he would place his "groundsheet-cum-cape" over my head if it rained whilst we were working in the fields. On the day of my birthday he brought to work a tablet of luxury toilet soap. "Appee birthday" he managed to say as he handed it to me. Apparently he had saved up his soap allowance in order to buy my gift.

The news of the war in Europe was encouraging and it seemed it was just a matter of time before the Germans capitulated. I had gradually come to terms with the situation of working alongside a German and I even handed Paul the occasional bar of chocolate and a packet of cigarettes. Physically I kept at a distance from Paul but late one afternoon as we walked back to the farm, side by side, he casually took hold of my hand, raised it to his mouth and kissed it. I turned, looked up at him and shook my head. Not a word passed between us but he got the message because it was the first and last time he made a pass at me. In fact, we became good friends and worked really well together. We spent endless days hoeing mangold seedlings until if felt like our backs would break and our hands were covered with the calluses and blisters. It was such a large area. Finally, the boss turned up one day with Pansy and the horsehoe. I was surprised when he asked Paul to lead the horse and I continued hand hoeing. Mr Edwards explained to Paul that the horse must be led in a straight line so that he himself could guide the hoe between the rows of young shoots. Then he signalled that he was ready to start. Paul grasped the reins and led Pansy forward but the horse had a mind of her own – Paul was a strange handler to her and she made off at full pelt across the field, dragging Paul on with her, taking the horse hoe with the boss trying to hang on to the steering handles, right across the field. By the time they got Pansy under control many mangolds had been up rooted along with the weeds. That plan was abandoned for the day and, as the master unhitched the horse and led her home, Paul resumed hand hoeing alongside me.

Early in nineteen forty-four a German aircraft, having been targeted and hit, limped away from the flak after action over either Exeter or Plymouth. Finally it crashed in a field across the valley killing the two-man crew. The explosion had left a huge crater and the unfortunate airmen had been buried respectfully in the graveyard at the Church in Upottery. Mr Edwards tried to explain this to Paul who indicated that he would like to visit the graves, and so one morning instead of going about the normal work day, the boss took Paul down tot he village on the pretext of having Pansy shod at the village smithy's. Apparently Paul picked some wild flowers from the hedgerows en route and whilst Pansy was having her new shoes fitted he and Mr Edwards visited the grave leaving the flowers as a token of respect for the two ex-Luftwaffe crew. In time when war was long over these men were exhumed and taken back to the fatherland for burial near their loved ones.

One day Paul asked permission to cut off a little hair from each of the horses' tails. This accomplished he wrapped it in newspaper and carried it back to camp without any explanation. Weeks later he proudly presented the boss and me with a small parcel each and inside we discovered expertly made clothes brushes – the results of his acquisition of the horse hair.

RURAL HUMOUR

It was really great meeting up with Kathy again and we joined in with village life together. I accepted the invitations of a couple of farmer's sons and entered into a few light-hearted flirtatious liaisons but they were little more than platonic as far as my feelings went. I did succumb to an occasional kiss and cuddle but my heart was not in it.

One night Lewis, a local farmer's son, was escorting me home from the Whist Drive. It was quite a long walk from the Village Hall to Kitts Farm and when we reached Down Elms a ghostly, pure white, headless, legless apparition floated across the lane in front of us and disappeared into the plat opposite the house.

"It's the lads," Lewis remarked, "Taking the mick because I'm seeing you home."

As we passed the gate to the plat Lewis climbed over and peered behind the cowsheds but he couldn't see anyone. Consequently we passed by and continued our journey.

The following evening I decided to go over to the Symes's to sort out the saga of the spectre we had witnessed on the previous evening, but before I had chance to ask questions Bessie told me how she had hung out her washing the day before and had left it on the line overnight. "Can't mek it out," she said, "My Ed's best white shirt were still there on the line exactly where I had left it the night afore but when I went out to check if it were dry this morning it were covered in cow shit."

It dawned on me what had taken place. One of the village lads had unpegged the shirt, put it on and glided across the lane in front of Lewis and me as we strolled by. But I played the innocent and never divulged what had happened or who the culprits were. My secrecy was all in vain because the lads thought it was hilariously funny and soon everybody for miles around knew of the escapade. It took years to live it down.

Art, the thirty nine years old brother of Mrs Edwards, still a bachelor, had from time to time invited me to see a film at the Devonia Cinema (now the auction rooms on the bank of the River Gissage) in Honiton. I had made excuses time after time to avoid accepting mainly because of the age difference but eventually, fearing I would cause offence by my continual refusals, I agreed to go on condition that we met Kathy on the way there. This was all arranged and off we three cycled into Honiton to see an Abbott and Costello film. On the return journey I began to get cold feet and cowardly suggested that Art see Kathy back to Wellsprings Farm because the farm lane was dark and isolated but Kathy protested that she had taken the route alone many times before and she had no qualms whatsoever. We bade her "Goodnight" before continuing a further couple of miles back to Kitts. On arrival I propped up my bicycle in its usual place in the wagon house and Art did likewise. To my utter dismay he then put his arms around me and drew me close to him.

"Micky," he said, "Will 'ee do I a vavour?

Full of suspicion I asked, "What's the favour?"

"Doan 'ee let our Sis know I've ask 'ee out," he requested.

"And why not?" I further queried.

"Well, if muther vound out I'd been out wi' a girl, her'd go mad," came his explanation.

"Sorry, Art," I said pushing past him, "If you're so scared and ashamed of me, forget it!" I called as I trounced in through the farmhouse door.

A man of almost forty years afraid that his mother would object to him having a lady friend! I just couldn't believe what he had said but I kept his secret and didn't tell a soul. Kathy knew, of course, and she also can recall that evening. From time to time I met Art in the course of my work – he would bring his tractor over to carry out certain jobs for his brother-in-law jobs which necessitated the use of a tractor such as seed drilling or reaping and binding but I pretended that our little rendezvous had never come to pass.

Kathy had an American boyfriend and on one occasion I was asked to make up a foursome, a kind of blind date. I agreed and we all had a pleasant stroll through Pine Park in Honiton. The boys took some snapshots and we opted to go to The Red Cow for a drink. At that time the Red cow consisted of just one small bar and it was full to capacity when we arrived – we were packed in like sardines. It was here that I tried to smoke my first (and last) cigarette. It was a Camel and the experience left me wondering, even to this day, what pleasure or satisfaction most people derived from this pastime. To this day I have never been tempted to take up this habit.

I met this young man on a couple of dates when we danced at the Mackarness Hall or had a coffee and doughnut in the Doughnut Dugout at the rear of the Dolphin Hotel but on our last date, he walked off in a huff when I refused him sex. I had no regrets. I just collected my bicycle from the stables behind the Kings Arms (the Landlord had previously agreed that I could leave it there whenever I was in Honiton) then I cycled home.

By this time I had become more involved with the local activities and

The New Dolphin Hotel as it is today. During the war its former ballroom became The Doughnut Dugout.

was beginning to feel more accepted by the villagers. It helped greatly that Mr and Mrs Edwards never lost the opportunity to sing my praises. "Hers a rippin' maid to work," he would declare as he broadcast to one and all what a reliable, hardworker I was, on many occasions to my embarrassment. This was the ultimate accolade in the farming community.

My trips to Honiton and Exeter almost petered out until the only time I visited was if I needed any specific shopping. Most things were obtainable at the farmhouse door. A medley of tradespeople called. They ranged from two bakers; a butcher; Mr Hemsley who had a hardware shop in New Street, Honiton and delivered paraffin; Hoskins, the outfitters; Bassetts the grocers; Manley's the chemists, also of New Street; the egg collector; Mrs Layzell with second-hand clothing; the milk lorry, of course and even Gypsy Manley who would buy and sell most things. He always took on the rabbit and moleskins. We stretched out the moleskins on a board and he paid a full six pence for a good, undamaged skin.

JACK

At the beginning of April I met a young RAF man at the village dance called Jack. He was stationed at Smeathorpe Aerodrome just outside Upottery. Jack was a particularly handsome man but quite the opposite to the men I had previously been attracted to. He was almost albino in colouring, that is, he had white-blonde hair and the palest of blue eyes and he sported a wonderful tan. We became quite fond of each other as we courted over the following three months. He monopolised my every free minute and we met on every possible occasion when our respective duties allowed and we became very good friends as well as sweethearts. Jack was ten years older than me and was very quiet in nature. His idea of a good time was a quiet

91

Land Army friend, Kay, on leave in Morcambe in 1945, and (above), with ther author high up in the Dolomites, in Italy, during a shared holiday to the Lake Garda area in 2004.

drink and a meal in one of the villages. If I was off duty on Saturdays he would sometimes meet me and we would ride our bicycles to Honiton in the afternoon. We'd lunch at either the Carlton Restaurant, Gill's Cafe (now Somerfields) or the Highland Fling (now the Boston Tea Party). After looking around the shops we would cycle back to the Sidmouth Arms for a quiet drink. We rarely attended a dance and on the odd occasion when we did I didn't enjoy myself. He watched my every move seemingly begrudging me the pleasure of dancing with my friends and I felt stifled.

VICTORY IN EUROPE – VE DAY – 8TH MAY 45
The news from Europe became increasingly exciting and then it happened. The Germans had capitulated; the war in Europe was over; Victory was ours – VE Day – May 8th. The quiet valley suddenly became alive with the roundelay of church bells ringing.

When war had been declared we were told that all the church bells across the nation would remain silent. Should we hear them ring during wartime it would be as an indication that the enemy had invaded and landed on our shores. Fortunately that never came to pass and now after five long years the war was over and once more the air was filled with a joyful reassuring sound.

"Day off, today, Mick," Mr Edwards called when we had finished the morning milking and the churns were lifted onto the stand awaiting collection.

"But doan'ee be minded to run off home yet a while. Them Japs have ta be put in their place yet." It really was a joyous day. Even the weather was wonderful.

"The powers that be" at the centre of social arrangements together with Lord and Lady Sidmouth had made plans for celebrations prior to the end of war treaty. The entire population attended a Service of Thanksgiving in St Mary's Church in the afternoon and preparations had been made for a huge party in the Manor Room that evening. Between these events the Edwards family and me rested in anticipation of a hectic night ahead. What a great party we had! The menfolk had built a huge bonfire at the top of Aller Hill; farmers donated barrel upon barrel of cider and the ladies of the parish really excelled themselves with their whole hams, cheeses, and scrumptious cakes. Devon Splits in abundance were heaped high with home-made jams and clotted cream and every surface of the Manor Room kitchen was filled to capacity.

We sang at full throttle that evening as we milked the cows – even the boss joined in with my crazy songs and then we went indoors to wash, change and pamper ourselves in readiness for the evenings activities.

Jack called to collect me later and everyone was surprised when I came downstairs. They were expecting me to be dressed up in my glamorous red dress but I had decided that this was the one time in my life when I should wear my uniform with pride.

The Sidmouth Arms was packed to the hilt when we arrived there shortly before nine o'clock. Drink was flowing fast and free and most people were already shiny-eyed and merry from over indulging. A radio blared our popular songs and we all joined in the singing. What a wonderful carefree day!

Eddie Selway was already in full swing as we entered the Manor Room and we danced the Lambeth Walk, the Palais Glide and the Hokey-Cokey non stop until we were fit to drop. All the delicious food was free and hogshead replaced hogshead as people took their fill of cider. I must have become quite tipsy myself because the activities gradually became hazy. We were all hugging and kissing each other with delight and relief and the revelries carried on all night – the party had no beginning and no ending.

It was precisely five o'clock the next morning when I rolled home. I simply went up to my room, changed into my dungarees and walked straight down to the courtyard, brought the cows in and started milking.

When dinner was over that day we were all very tired so Mr Edwards decided we needed another afternoon off in order to recuperate – we all went to bed, arose to attend to the necessary evening chores, had tea and toddled off to bed again where we remained until the following morning when life got back to normal. Every city, town and village throughout the land celebrated the end of hostilities in Europe in the dancing, singing, hugging and lots of fun.

Some three months later VJ Day (Victory in Japan) did not appear to warrant the same atmosphere. It was truly wonderful that the cruel, brutal Japanese had been vanquished but the horrors of the treatment of prisoners they held and particularly those who had suffered and perished during the enforced building of the Burma Railway were instilled in our minds. Other factors too which affected our senses were that this war seemed far removed from us on the opposite side of the globe. Not lease of all was the devastation and death brought about by the explosions of the Atomic Bombs on Nagasaki and Hiroshima. Giving this latter horror deep thought I believe that, devastating as it was, in the long term this decision to drop the bombs did save countless lives. It brought the war with its attending atrocities to an abrupt end and who knows how many more lives could have been lost had it dragged on and on interminably. This I realise is a debatable subject.

RUTH'S DILEMMA

I wrote many letters during my weekday evenings. I still corresponded with Bill Walmsley, Bill Routledge, Walter, Arthur in addition to girlfriends I had left up in Lancashire and to relatives. Arthur's letter writing to me did not flag one iota and now he was looking forward to coming home from Aden. The only Land Girl I had remained in contact with, discounting Kathy, was Ruth and I was both shocked and dismayed when she wrote to tell me that she was pregnant. She had continued a liaison with Ken Graves a US Sailor based at Dunkeswell and apparently he was the father-to-be.

"Don't worry Micky," she wrote, "Ken is standing by me and we're hoping to get married before the baby is born."

She then informed me that she would be leaving the Women's Land Army and returning to her home in Oldham. This was followed by her new address. I had to some extent regretted never having slept with Stoney despite our passionate love-making but now I thanked God that we had abstained and I now realised how wise we had been, poor Ruth!

The stigma attached to being an unmarried mother in those times was absolutely unimaginable but what was done, was done.

Over the following weeks I bought wool and knitted some baby clothes. Clothing coupons had to be forfeited even for wool but I managed to scrape a few together and in addition I bought a large flannelette sheet, which I made into four cot sheets. Ruth was very appreciative.

DECEPTION

When we had finished breakfast one morning Mrs Edwards asked me to stay behind, as there was something she wished to discuss with me in private. Whatever had I done that warranted such a request?

"Now don't take this the wrong way, Micky, but there is something I feel you ought to know," she commenced.

"Yes?" I enquired still racking my brain as to what it could possibly be.

"Well, Cecil Stevens knows you and Jack are courting and he informed us that Jack is a married man with two children."

Cecil's father farmed land adjoining the airfield at Smeathorpe and I knew that the family socialised with some of the airmen stationed there. I was dumbfounded and wanted to refute this suggestion but then I realised it was a possibility.

"I'm absolutely speechless," was all I could say, "I'll hear what he has to say for himself."

Mrs Edwards was my friend and confidant. She had been a shoulder to cry on when Stoney disappeared and a mentor on other matters in my private life. I knew that she had my interests at heart when disclosing this scandal to me.

Jack came over that very evening and I lost no time in asking him outright if he was married

"No," was all he said

"Show me some proof," I demanded.

With this he produced an RAF identity card from the breast pocked of his tunic and handed it to me without uttering a word. Sure enough the section, which stated "single, married, divorced," was followed by a large "S". I handed back the card but thought he looked rather uncomfortable. What more could I do?

There was nothing more I could do or say and so I acted as if the subject had never been broached. Mrs Edwards was distinctly puzzled and quite apologetic when I told her of the outcome. This, as it eventually turned out, was not the end of the subject.

Love At First Sight

One fine evening in early June, Jack called for me as usual and we walked down to the village pub. By now I was starting to find this routine monotonous. I was almost eighteen years old and I was missing the company of younger people, the dancing and having fun. We sat on a bench in the small bar in the Sidmouth Arms talking. Jack had placed an arm around my waist as he hugged me to him. Suddenly the peace was disturbed as a crowd of young people burst into the pub – it was the Symes family who, it turned out, were on their way to a party at Eddie Selway's cottage on Aller Farm.

And then I saw him – an extremely tall, slim, handsome man in naval uniform emerged from the crowd and peered inquisitively into the room. Our eyes met and locked. The spell was only broken when he wickedly winked his eye and I looked away. But the damage was done. I had no idea who this man could be but I knew I had to meet him again.

The Symes party just had one drink and then moved on. The following day I told Mrs Edwards of my encounter with a sailor but she, too, could not fathom out who from the locality was in the Navy.

Normal life resumed but at teatime a few days later Mr Edwards remarked with a mischievous glint in his eye, "Young Shire has been up and down our lane twice today. Wonder what he's looking for?"

"That'll be your sailor," Mrs Edwards had fathomed out, "forgot all about him. He's been away so long and I know he's been wounded but I remember he joined the navy years ago."

I lost interest in Jack from that moment on but what excuse could I give for bringing our relationship to a close. In actual fact the problem solved itself but not in a way I had expected. Rumours still persisted about him being married and I didn't know what action to take. Then one evening when he kissed me goodnight in the Wagon House the truth came out.

"Micky, I've been posted to a station near Poole in Dorset and I want you to come with me," he blurted out.

"Is this a proposal then?" I queried.

"Well, yes, in a way, eventually," he stuttered then, "when my divorce comes through."

"Oh!" I came back, "and since when did a single man need to get a divorce?"

I was only half listening as he proceeded to tell me the usual drift about his marriage and how they had separated eighteen months ago and that he now wanted to start anew with me. I could leave the Land Army, move in with him, he would look after me .... on and on and on it went.

Now my own thoughts were leading me in another direction. I was free to follow my heart. I told Jack in no uncertain terms what I thought of him and made it clear I never wanted to see him again then stormed off indoors.

I was filled with relief. I realised I had been searching for a loop hole for some considerable time whereby I could bring this association to an end and now it had happened right out of the blue.

HAYMAKING

Mr Edwards had predicted that, weather permitting, he would mow his first meadow on the ninth of June.

"Vathur allus said 'Frank, thees not go var wrong if thee start thee haymaking on't' ninth of June', and ee baint been wrong zo var," he commented.

June the ninth dawned and it was a beautiful day, dry and sunny, so out he went after breakfast with Pansy and the mowing machine and cut the first grass of nineteen forty five. Meals were carried out to him because once he commenced, he refused to stop until the field had been completed.

That was the start and the following weeks meant even longer working days for the weather was superb. When the grass was ready to be turned I would take Bob or Frolic out with the swath turner, then later the tedder which threw and tossed the hay in all directions. Next came the Horserake which ridged the now dry hay into thick, long, neat lines. We usually raked these rows into regimented heaps equidistant from each other but occasionally we would put the sweep (rake) into service. Mr Edwards was not too keen on using the sweep – upending it at specific intervals was extremely hard work. Using horses meant that no border grass was wasted (as it is when tractors are used) and I would spend a lot of time raking in the edge of the fields with my wide, wooden-toothed hay rake. Finally when the boss decreed that the hay was ready it would be manually thrown up into the large wagon with its retaining 'lades' (a gate-like structure fixed at an obtuse angle at the back and front ends of the wagon). Jess Hunt, the master rick builder would be upon the wagon putting the hay about whilst Mr Edwards and I threw up the loose hay using a two-pronged hay fork. The hay was carted to the hayshed where it was again transferred manually from wagon to shed. Jess taught me how to lay a rick so that it would not topple or spew out and I could not have had a finer tutor. When the shed was filled we built a free-standing rick inside the entrance to Pitfield. When it was completed we would fence it off, let it settle for a while then employ

'Ole man Moon, the Thatcher, to rough thatch it. Mr Moon was in his eighties and amazingly spry for his age. He caused great amusement when he said to me, "Lordy, if I were sixty years younger I'd stiffer up my feathers to you, maid." He always had a naughty twinkle in his eye.

And so our haymaking progressed, field after field, week in week out, working all the daylight hours and more. My hands were rough and callused as a result of the relentless use of the hayrake and the pitching fork. Work always took priority over social activities. In fact, no whist drives or social events were promoted during this season – harvest home was the first celebratory event when haymaking and harvesting had all been completed.

Despite the urgency in getting the crops in, Mr Edwards stuck by his religious ethics and only essential care of the livestock was undertaken on Sundays. Even if a field was 'ready' he would wait until Monday to bring it in, praying the good weather would hold out. As always neighbour assisted neighbour and when the day's work was completed, all hands were invited in to supper – the usual excellent fare and the usual abundance of cider.

The weather was hot and the need for fluid continuous and it was always cider that was placed in a cool place beneath the hedgerow. One night when all had left for their respective homes I felt quite tipsy as I lit my candle and prepared to climb the stairs. Mrs Edwards, seeing I was a little unsteady, substituted my own bicycle lamp for the candle fearing for my safety. The outcome was that I spent ages trying to blow out my battery lamp!!

One Sunday evening I strolled over to Down Elms, and John, one of the sons, suggested we go down to the village for a drink and a game of skittles. I agreed and just as we were about to leave in walked my sailor. He was in civilian garb but he still looked great to me. John was apparently his buddy and he invited him to accompany us. It really was love a first sight for both Alan and me. When our eyes met the message was quite clear for both of us and we were only aware of each other. We all spent a pleasant evening in the Sidmouth Arms and when we reached Down Elms and John said, "goodnight", Alan continued on with me over to the farm. Despite the underlying feelings that first evening Alan just leaned towards me and placed a gentle kiss on my lips. Before leaving he asked if he could take me to Honiton Fair on the following Saturday evening. We arranged to meet at a certain road junction under Bob Shute's Cover near the A30 road.

I could scarcely wait until Saturday. I knew so little about him other than where he lived and that he was on convalescence leave due to being wounded in both legs, whilst serving on HMS Colombo, which was escorting a Malta Convoy in the Mediterranean. Being so busy that week meant that the time flew by and at last Saturday came round.

It was one of those magical mornings, fresh and peaceful, and as usual I was bewitched by the beauty of my surroundings. A mist hung low over the River Otter giving it a mystical aura as I brought the cows in for milking. Courtyard work completed and the herd happily grazing I went in to have my breakfast.

"Cissie tells I thees got plans vor today, Maid," Mr Edwards appeared to be uncomfortable as he spoke. Sorry, Mick, but there's two fields of hay dry and ready – means another long day. Can't risk letting it lie til Monday. Weather forecast's dodgy."

That was all he said. I could sense an underlying apology but I had no choice. The hay needed hauling in and that was that. But how could I get the message to Alan? I couldn't keep my promise and meet him – I just hoped he would understand the position I was in.

As the boss had predicted it turned out to be another long day. Jess Hunt and Ernie Joyce (a labourer who worked on Rookery Farm, our neighbour) lent a hand and as always the work was hot and hard but the atmosphere was jovial. We had to continue after having our tea.

Whilst pitching hay up into the wagon I happened to glance up and had a wonderful surprise when Alan, looking so very handsome in his uniform came strolling down the field. Awkwardly I tried to explain why I hadn't put in an appearance at Bob Shute's. He stopped me by gently placing his hand over my mouth and reassuring me that he could well see the situation I was in. Discarding his tie, hat and jacket and loosening his shirt he proceeded to work alongside me until every heap of dry hay was safely gathered in. I should have realised that, bred, born and reared hereabouts, he knew the country code.

It was quite a jolly party in the farmhouse that night. We didn't get in until after ten o'clock but then the feast began. There is always an air of relaxation and satisfaction after a job well accomplished and the atmosphere that evening was wonderful. The boss was well pleased and he was in a very humorous mood making a joke of everything. The smile on Mrs Edwards' face was incessant as she urged us to tuck in to supper. Mrs Joyce had joined us with Doris, their young curly mopped daughter and even old Mrs Hunt had made the effort to come over the lane to help Mrs Edwards prepare the food. After several mugs of cider old Jess was in festive mood and full of nonsense. He sang, he joked and when he started to do a dance, a kind of cross between ballet and a clog-dance, his wife considered it was time to call it a day.

"I've got something special for you, Jess," Mrs Edwards informed the old man. "Your special cheese."

With this she went up into the diary and struggled back carrying a huge, whole home-made cheese. The blue vein was apparent when she cut into it but so were the maggots. Jess maintained that the finest, tastiest cheese was the one with maggots, and, yes, he ate the maggots along with the cheese. Aagh!!

Alan stayed by my side constantly and when the guests had left and the Edwards' family were ready for bed, I strolled partway down the lane with him. We paused by the five-barred gate to the Lower Orchard; he took me in his arms and kissed me as I had never been kissed before. The memory of that kiss remains with me; the memory will never leave me. My fate was sealed and later he told me that his reaction and feelings had been exactly the same.

I often think I have been extraordinarily lucky to have had two great loves in my lifetime because I loved Alan with the same passion and intensity that I had felt for Stoney – they have been the only men to have lit a real spark in my heart. One I lost for ever but the other remains with me after almost sixty years and will do so "until death do us part". Our relationship has been very hard, rocky at times (when I have really hated him) but never, ever have we fallen out of love.

Henceforth Alan and I were inseparable, our respective duties allowing. Whenever he came home on leave and I was at liberty, we were together. We didn't need to be entertained, in fact, we spent many hours strolling the field paths and country lanes or ambling along the river banks, holding hands and occasionally turning towards each other for a long passionate kiss and a cuddle. He knew that I loved the wild violets which in those times grew in abundance on the hedgerows so he would pick a small bunch whilst I sat on the river bank dangling my feet in the water. He would bind the short stems with a blade of couch grass and either hand them to me or tuck them in my hair over my ear. He once tied them to the drawstring at the neck of my dress and those I kept for many years pressed between the pages of a thick book.

Our courtship was full of romance and I sensed he appreciated the contrast of life there and then to the hell he had suffered whilst on active service. Coming from the city there were lots of things I hitherto did not know about the countryside. He pointed out different animal tracks and taught me the names of all the birds and even how to distinguish their songs. He made a whistle from a certain type of grass and pointed out a heron and a kingfisher. It was a magical time.

Of course, there were other times when we attended the whist drives, which he loved, and we occasionally went to a dance, which he loathed (he had two left feet). On my Saturday afternoon off we would cycle into Honiton. It was market day which meant he met up with many of his friends for a pint and a 'yarn' whilst I checked out the shops. At seven o'clock we always made for the Cosy Café at the west end of Honiton, at the bottom of the dip. Here we tucked in to sausage, eggs, and chips before returning to one or other of the hotels. Here he loved to play darts, table skittles, alley skittles, cards or dominoes so I would stay by his side and give my support.

Occasionally he would come over to Kitts Farm and help me to milk the cows in order that I would be able to finish up earlier. Strangely Ferdinand didn't take to him making the motions of tupping at him if he passed.

Later Alan was transferred to Appledore in North Devon where he was placed in a civilian billet so he managed quite often to come home for a weekend.

HARVESTING
For me summer meant working the extra hours. There seemed to be little time between the completion of our haymaking and the beginning of the harvesting. Compared to the vast acreage's of corn grown nowadays, the amount we grew was negligible, so harvesting was not such a long drawn out job as haymaking. We needed to be self sufficient as far as we possibly could so that the amount we grew was relevant to our own needs for the sustenance and fattening of our livestock. We never sold any corn. Being a mixed farm we were expected to contribute to the country's larders by means of milk (dairy produce) and fatstock (pigs, sheep, lambs and fat steers). Poultry was another outlet as were the innumerable quantities of rabbits which the boss caught and sold.

Threshing day on a neighbouring farm.

Land Girls harvesting with a reaper and binder.

A good upright crop of corn (oats, barley, wheat, maize) meant that Mr Edwards could hire the services of a reaper and binder which cut the stalks and bound them into sheaves before ejecting them. My job was to pick up these sheaves and stook them for drying out. They would then be ricked until threshing time came around when the grains were separated from the straw and chaff. That year one field of corn had flattened – it lay along the ground – so this meant cutting it by a hand scythe and manually tying it up in bundles before stooking. The continual swinging, rhythmically, back and forth, of the scythe brought into play muscles I never knew I had. My shoulders and arms felt fit to drop off from the unrelenting aching and I got even more blisters on my hands, hardened as they had become. Yet still I thrived on my work and loved every minute of it. I could always see the rewards of my labours, which gave great satisfaction. The end product was always gratifying.

Whatever task I was asked to perform on this farm, I carried out to the best of my ability but there was one thing I flatly refused to be associated with and that was the snaring and trapping of rabbits. The least popular method for catching rabbits was shooting because although it caused less suffering, the lead shot could spread in the tissues and ruin the meat. Rabbiting by shooting was mainly for sport. In my estimation the other two methods were downright cruel. The wire snares did not always kill the quarry outright sometimes even cutting through to the body causing prolonged untold agony. Similarly the gin trap mainly caught the animals by the legs partly severing them. When Mr Edwards took me around the hedges to release these unfortunate animals he instructed me on how to break their necks by holding them upside down by the hind legs and sharply striking their necks using the side of the hand. To me these procedures were too abhorrent for words and I told Mr Edwards that in no way was I prepared to take part in such atrocities.

My feelings were respected.

VICTORY IN JAPAN – VJ DAY – 20TH AUGUST 1945

All of a sudden, quite out of the blue, it was announced that the war was over. The Japanese Emperor, Hirohito, had succumbed and agreed to unconditional surrender following the devastation caused by just two bombs. It seemed incredible at that time that a single bomb could completely wipe out a city. They were, of course, the powerful, destructive Atom bombs – one obliterated Hiroshima and the other flattened Nagasaki. They were hitherto unknown quantities and the magnitude of the effect on Japan was enough to persuade the Emperor to throw in the towel.

It was an extremely horrific raid but then the Japanese were themselves cruel, barbaric and very, very stubborn and the action of the United States of America curtailed a war which would have continued endlessly until every far eastern country and island which the Japs had occupied and annihilated had been fought for individually and freed from their tyranny and liberated. This would have resulted in much more untold misery and death.

So we celebrated VJ day but in a soberly fashion. At last all hostilities had ceased. Soon His Majesty's Forces were being repatriated ready for demobilisation.

A BOLT FORM THE BLUE

The corn we grew was ground to a meal and mixed with ground roots, mainly mangolds, and along with hay, and 'good' straw fed to the dairy herd when necessary. 'Poor' straw was used for their bedding. Processed animal foods such as dairy nuts, sheep nuts and pig meal were rationed out according to numbers and did not amount to large quantities. We pulled the mangold, cut off the leaves and stored them in a huge cave on the lee side of a hedge in Roundabout, where they had been grown. He cave was covered with straw and then fenced off.

We had just about finished pulling the mangolds, which turned out to be an exceptionally good crop. Freddie Smith had left me a letter, which I could tell was from my mother. I had placed it on the sideboard with the intention of reading it during my dinner break assuming it to be the usual news of the family and home. Whilst Mrs Edwards served up the dinner I opened my letter and it came as quite a shock to read that mum was suffering from some abdominal problem relating to a major operation she had previously undergone. It appeared that she seriously needed me back home as soon as possible. Her surgery had been of a serious nature and she had been lucky to have recovered from it and so I felt duty bound to apply for a temporary transfer. Haymaking and harvesting had been completed so I had no qualms about leaving the Edwards' in the lurch.

I wrote to the Women's Land Army headquarters and applied for a temporary transfer for about two months suggesting that I be placed on some farm in the Blackburn area. Within a short period of time my reply arrived explaining that I had been allocated a short term position at a farm on the outskirts of Blackburn bordering Darwen Moor. It was essential that I lived in at the farm from Monday to Friday leaving me free to go home to Rishton each weekend.

I was gutted at the thought of leaving Kitts Farm, the family and most of all, Alan, but my train pass duly arrived along with the date when I would be expected to put in an appearance at the farm of Mr and Mrs Thistlewaite.

Mr and Mrs Edwards were very understanding; they knew how much I loved my mother and they sympathised with my dilemma telling me to hurry back when all was settled. It proved a much more difficult task convincing Alan that I had to sort things out at home for my own peace of mind. I said all my goodbyes and set out for Taunton Station and eventually, home.

My mother was very relieved to have me home and she looked very pale and her features were drawn. She had hoped I would have been able to work from home, commuting daily, but I explained what my orders were and that an exceptionally early start to my day left me no alternative but to board at the farm throughout the weekdays. After a lovely weekend spent with her and my two younger sisters, I once again packed my case and reported to my new employer on Monday morning.

My new duties were totally opposed to the work I had become accustomed to. To my dismay, I was not allowed anywhere near an animal except for the old mare, which pulled the milk float around the streets of Blackburn. Yes my new job was to deliver milk to the people who dwelt in that area of the city. In addition I was to keep the huge dairy and all the milking utensils sterilised and spotless – quite a contrast to what I had been accustomed to. There were no bottles of milk with which I had to deal. Customers left their milk jugs or canisters on their doorsteps from whence I picked them up and carried them back to the milk float, horsedrawn of course. Here I would measure out the required amount of milk using three different metal measures – gill, pint and quart – which hooked over the rim of the milkchurn. The jug plus contents were then returned to the doorstep. I'd ring the bell and the customer would relieve me of the jug. At certain houses a metal flask with fitted lid would be left. In such instances I would replace the filled container on the doorstep ring the bell and leave.

I started work very early each morning and would meet with the "knocker-uppers" – people paid to knock on the bedroom windows using a long pole thus awakening the residents who would open the window and shout, indicating that they had roused. Most mornings I would also meet up with the gas-lighter man. Each night around dusk he would go around the streets with a hook-ended pole with which he pulled down a cross lever releasing the supply of gas and igniting it thus lighting up the street gas lamps. I usually encountered him each morning when he would pull the opposite side of the cross lever thus cutting off the gas and extinguishing the lamp.

I had no difficulties in serving the correct customers. I had been given a list but my old mare knew where to stop better than I did and as soon as I had made a delivery and was up in the cart again she would immediately trundle on. She knew the route and always paused at the correct houses.

I would arrive back at the farm before one o'clock, unload the empty churns, stable and feed the horse before going in to dinner. The food and cooking was not a patch on that to which I had become accustomed in Devon but it was still good compared to the standards in wartime.

The farmer was a quiet, gentle man, ready to answer any queries I put to him but his wife was extremely jealous – she watched me like a hawk. The cowman warned me of this right from the start. Seemingly my predecessor had been asked to move on simply for laughing and joking with Mr Thistlethwaite. I soon realised that she was the boss and I was almost neurotic when it came to working beside her husband, scarcely daring to look at him. The atmosphere was so very different from the one at Kitts Farm where we had been such a happy family. Mr Thistlethwaite was a totally respectable; faithful husband or so it seemed and I never knew him to give his wife any grounds whatsoever for her jealousy and mistrust.

My duties after dinner were the cleaning of the huge dairy sterilising all the utensils used for milking and for the milk deliveries. Lastly I scrubbed the floor and scoured the milk float itself. By the time I had finished, all the buckets would be lined up on a long shelf, all clean and gleaming and the churns, coolers and sieves etc. were immaculate. My working day usually ended at around half past four when I was free for the remainder of the day. What a difference form the long hours I was used to in Devon!

My bedroom was large and luxuriously furnished with hand-hooked home-made woollen rugs (Mrs Thistlethwaite's hobby) and soft, downy eiderdown.

Yet for all of this I was not content there. I missed my animals so much. I missed Pansy, Frolic and Bob. I missed Whiteface, Bluebell, Penelope and the other cows. I missed Watch, Towser and Sport. I even missed Ferdinand. But most of all I missed the Edwards and yearned for Alan. Thank goodness I was to return eventually.

It was obvious that my mother was far from well but I also suspected that she was having problems with her partner. I had never liked him. In fact my main reason for enlisting in the Women's Land Army was to get away from him and I had hoped that by doing so their relationship would improve but that had so obviously not happened. There was nothing I could do – it was mother's place to make decisions about her private life – her choice. Much of my free time at weekends was spent in helping with the housework and laundry. Gradually she seemed to improve. The colour had come back to her cheeks to some extent and she seemed more like her old self. She was not entirely happy about my impending return to Devon but I told her that the following Spring she was to come down and stay with me and if not I would make arrangements with Mrs Joyce for her to stay there. She would be only a few hundred yards up the lane from the farmhouse.

I had written several letters to Alan and I was hurting so much because he had not contacted me in any way – I really thought he had walked out of my life – I had lost him.

It was two weeks before I was due to go back to Kitts that I received a phone call from Arthur. He was about to be demobbed and was home on leave in Manchester and he asked that we arrange to meet. What had I got to lose now? He promised to pick me up from the coach when I arrived in Manchester and I was invited by his parents to stay with them for a couple of days. It was pleasant to see him and his family again after such a long time but I knew from the moment we met again that there was no future together for Arthur and me. There was no spark and it was like welcoming home a big brother. I was taken aback when I realised that his family assumed that we were planning a reconciliation. His mother even displayed china and household articles, which she had put aside for us. Now I realised I must put this idea to rest once and for all. I politely informed Arthur and his parents that I would not be pressurised into a situation, which I would likely regret in the future. I thanked them for their hospitality and excused myself as I set out for the coach station and my journey home to Rishton. I did feel sorry for Arthur. He was a placid, laid back kind of guy and I hated hurting him. He insisted on seeing me safely on the coach and said he would write to me once I returned to Devon. Would he ever give up?

The following days dragged on endlessly. I had lost interest in my job and had become quite depressed. Mr Thistlethwaite tried to persuade me to stay on permanently. He contacted the Women's Land Army HQ and they in turn suggested I abandon my plans to resume my previous employment but I was adamant. I reminded one and all that the present arrangement was a temporary placement and that I was committed to returning to work for Mr Edwards.

This resolve was strengthened when shortly before I was due to return, I received a letter from Mrs Edwards begging me to hasten back. Mr Edwards had walked with a limp, the result of a nasty kick whilst he was breaking in a horse and now it turned out that he had fallen and fractured the same leg. Mrs Edwards and Gladys were struggling to cope with the essential work whilst caring for the boss. They were depending on me to get back as soon as possible as I had promised. I had to honour my agreement with the Thistlethwaites but I returned to Upottery on the very weekend I had previously promised.

And still I hadn't heard from Alan!

What a welcome I received at the farm on my return. I walked back into that dingy, austere farmhouse and I was so pleased to be back. I could scarcely imagine that when I first arrived there I had cried myself to sleep most nights.

After the excitement had subsided I was happy to resume my working duties and immediately took over the care of the dairy herd and the other animals. Mad though it may appear, I put my arms around the neck of each cow when I milked them that evening and planted a kiss on each hairy cheek.

Shortly before I left Rishton I had written a letter to Alan despite the fact that he had seemingly cut me out of his life. My letter was not overly affectionate but I did tell him of my plans to return to Kitts Farm the following weekend. I also assured him that my feelings for him remained unchanged, but apparently there was neither letter nor message from him awaiting me. I decided that was all the chasing I was prepared to do; the ball was in his court now: I would not let him hurt my pride any more even though I was heartbroken.

I worked all day on the Sunday, mucking out and cleaning sheds, stables and stalls, then after tea I washed and changed into a dress with court shoes and walked the lane to revisit the Symes family and let them know I was back. They, too, were over the moon to hear the news and they knew that the Edwards had been struggling. We spent a lovely evening together as they wanted to know all about my work up in Lancashire and how my family were and in return I listened to all the latest village news and gossip. Nobody mentioned Alan.

I was about to retrace my steps back to Kitts and have an early night after all the excitement. There was bright moonlight, a beautiful crisp, clear night. I heard footsteps from the direction of Preston Farm then I saw the silhouette of a man. Then it dawned on me – it was Alan. Should I behave formally, aloof perhaps? I didn't have to decide, he did, for when he was within a few yards of me he just opened his arms wide and I rushed to him, tears streaming down my face as he moved towards me and enfolded me close. We just embraced each other for quite some time before we gazed at each other and our lips met in a magical kiss.

I was home at last.

No explanations were called for (they came later). We were just so happy to be back in each others arms again and in each others hearts. It was most certainly a happy Land Girl who climbed the stairs to bed that night.

Alan had to catch the early morning train on the following day back to his duties at Appledore. Life got back to normal fairly quickly. The boss was not able to do much as he tried to hobble around with his leg in a plaster cast. Fortunately it was a slack time of the year as far as essential work was concerned and Christmas was just around the corner. When I explained that I had invited m mother to come down for a holiday sometime in the Spring, Mrs Edwards was really delighted and agreed that she could share my room. I just wondered what my mother would think of it all.

CHRISTMAS

I looked forward to Christmas 1945 with some trepidation. It would be the first time in my life when I would be away from my home and family. To compensate I would hopefully be with Alan and by now the Edwards were also my family. Over the years my mother had decorated the home with paper garlands, baubles, holly, ivy and mistletoe until it resembled a fairy grotto. We always had a Christmas tree ornately dressed and lighted with colour candles, which clipped to the branches. The doors were open to one and all; relatives, friends and strangers, all were welcome, guests would either bring their ration books or contributed Christmas fare. Mother was an excellent cook so meals were tasty and succulent and, despite rationing, food was plentiful. She always spent several days beforehand baking mince pies and all kinds of fancy cakes.

There was no television but we were always well entertained with board games, cards, dominoes, beetles, charades and many other fun games peculiar to parties. Music and singing were always at the top of the agenda and

Joe Loss, Oscar Rabin, Esmundo Ros and Glen Miller were the favourites of the times. Most importantly were the filled pillowcases, which we excitedly opened on Christmas morning always overflowing with gifts despite the hard times. Every available space would be filled with bowls of nuts and fruit, boxes of dates and figs and dishes of mints and fruit drops. Aunts, uncles and cousins from far and wide dropped in on us and often stayed for days.

I soon realised that here at Upottery the celebrations would be more tranquil. Gladys and her mother collected holly which were covered in blood red berries and hung them over each picture and mirror but there was no decorated tree or garlands. As always there was an abundance of food most of which was home produced; Goose, Pheasant, chicken, beef, ham and even the secretly stashed, precious dried fruit was brought out to make delicious fruit cake. In addition the usual home made fruit pies were covered in cream.

Here Christmas Day celebrated the birth of Christ and was quiet and peaceful and Boxing Day was the day for jollification. All in all to me it appeared to have a Dickensian feel about it.

I was happy enough with Alan always close at hand. The New Year heralded a more stable future. The war had been won; soldiers, sailors and airmen were demobbed, reunited with their families endeavouring to take up the reins of civilian life. In general there was still a shortage of food and the services of the Women's Land Army were still required. Alan was still at Appledore and I still continued in my job here at Kitts Farm. We never talked of the future together – I was only eighteen and he was twenty and we had only known each other for seven months. We lived from day to day enjoying each other in those moments we shared.

A group of smiling Land Girls.

Another Year

A novelty evening and dance was held at the Manor Room on New Years Eve which we attended and enjoyed.

The following day dawned with a Winter wonderland. Snow had fallen overnight and it continued for days making it very difficult to get out and about on the farm. Layer covered layer and it became very deep. We had to cut hay from a rick near the River and so the boss and I set out taking a long ladder with us. I led the way with my head through the front rungs of the ladder, the sides resting on my shoulders and he brought up the rear in similar fashion carrying a sharpened hay knife wrapped in a hessian sack under his arm. We encountered virgin snow, deep and untrodden, as we wended our way down hill. Deciding to have some high jinks I speeded up the pace to a canter, zigzagging to and fro across the field. Mr Edwards had know alternative but to follow entrapped as he was with his head between the ladder rungs. He shouted, he swore, he hollered so loudly that the whole of the parish could hear him. Because of the snow the noise resounded up and down the valley and his expletives were heard far and wide I was later told. Mrs Edwards had been up the lane at a poultry house and she came running down the lane wondering what the hullabaloo was about and she laughed until tears rolled down her cheeks at the spectacle. Later it dawned on me that he had a newly repaired fracture and was still unstable on his feet – I should have known better.

He amused me greatly because before venturing outside in the snow he would put each leg into a sack bag and lace in up to his thighs with binder twine. This was 'so called' to prevent him from slipping but it had the reverse affect when the snow clung to the sole part of the sack, it became compressed and icy. It did not take long for the sacks to become completely clogged up making them very heavy so that he struggled to place one foot in front of the other.

School transport was disrupted due to the snow laden roads, which meant that for a while Gladys did not go to school. To amuse her, her father improvised a sledge. He used a sheet of corrugated galvanised metal and curved it upwards and inwards at the ends and all three of us would sit on it, one behind the other and shoot down Long Mead at speed, barely managing to stop at the bottom (we used our feet to brake) before crashing into the hedge. Great fun!!

The Symes family also had a home made wooden sledge slightly more sophisticated than ours. On moonlit nights we would take turns guiding it down a very steep slope in the plat and ending up in a gully. Sometimes the runners would strike a small ridge or mound hurtling us off in all directions. Four at a time could squeeze on to this "designer sledge".

One evening four of the Symes family and a young man who lived at Kingston Cottage went sledging with Alan and me when we happened to catch sight of Mr Hardiman, also from Kingston Cottage, staggering up to his house very much worse for drink. Altogether we chased after him and invited him to try out our sledge.

"I can't struggle down this lane again," he objected, and so we all lifted him bodily over the top of the hedgerow and carried him to the top of the slope and placed him in an upright position on our sledge.

"Ready?" we called to him.

"Right, do thee worst," he answered. So with this we gave the sledge a hard push sending it speeding towards the gully. Not having his full faculties he was unable to balance in an upright position and we were alarmed to see his head bumping the hard ground as the sledge whizzed downwards. Worse still when it came to a halt he made no sound nor movement. He just lay there inertly.

"Hell, we've killed him," yelled one of the Symes boys as we all scrambled down into the gully after him. He was still immobile when we reached him but he looked up at us and demanded, "Thees zent I down, ye buggers, now thees best ways carry I up."

It was all hands on deck as we lifted the sledge in an attempt to get him back up the steep incline, but part way up the slope somebody dropped their corner of the sledge and off he rolled and roly-polyed to the bottom once more. We abandoned any attempt to carry him up on the sledge but eventually, between us, we managed to get him to the top, then back over the hedgerow, dumping him in the lane from whence we had first approached him.

A DYING CRAFT

I had become fascinated whilst watching Jess Hunt lay a hedge, intrigued by the skill and knowledge required. At first it seemed just a case of pairing the hedgerow and laying a sapling at intervals along the surface of the hedge. One day when the snow had melted and the fields were once again green, Jess came over to start laying a short hedge in the field above the hayshed orchard. I asked the boss if I could go with him as a kind of apprentice and naturally my interest was rewarded. So laden with a spade, a shovel, paring hooks, two seasoned crooks and a lump hammer, Jess and I set out together.

I was rather puzzled when he bypassed the chosen hedge and carried on up into the wood above. "Now maid, we've got to pick out suitable crooks and binds," he said and pointed out thin branch growth which sported an arrow-like shape. These we cut out shaping them to form a crook, sharpening each end to a point. When Jess considered we had trimmed out enough he said, "Thees'll do vor now. We'll likely vind more as we trim out the hedge."

Next we sorted out some withy binds, a willow with a fibrous, bendable stem.

"These'll be just the job," he pointed to a part of the wood where an abundance of withy grew. I racked my brain in an effort to fathom out what these "withy ropes" were likely to be used for in the process of laying a hedge, without success.

"Whatever do we need these for, Jess?" I queried.

"I'll show 'ee later, maid, zactly how to use 'em but we tie up the wood vaggots with 'em," came his reply. "That'll do vor now."

He handed me a bundle of crooks then threw the withy binds over his shoulder. We set off back to the field and commenced the task.

"Now we pare the hedge, maid. Cut out all the wood except what I mark," he said, selecting specific trees from amongst the growth on top of the hedge and marking it with a cross, cut out with his pocket knife. The trees he chose were neither mature trees nor saplings but something between the two.

We started at opposite ends of the hedgerow and pared out the small growth using paring hook and a crook and the thicker, older trees we chopped off with the wood hook. I had become quite adept at slicing through a tree often with one stroke in a downward direction.

"Now, dowan 'ee go chopping into thee leg. Allas cut away vrom theesel'," he advised.

It took us the rest of the day to trim the hedge. The following day we started to tidy up. Jess was meticulously tidy which suited me. The large wood had to be trimmed and placed in a neat heap ready for hauling whilst the small wood was made into faggots with the brushwood at one end and the straight sticks at the other. Now I learned the purpose of the withy binds. A suitable length was cut, the end of which was twisted into a loop with the loose ends being wound back around itself.

This bind was then placed around the waist of the faggot and the straight end threaded through the loop. Next the bind was pulled again and again until the faggot was held in a very firm bundle then the loose end was wrapped and twisted back on itself to secure the bind tightly. These faggots were also placed in neat piles ready for loading and transporting down to the wood pile.

This completed, our attention turned once more to the marked trunks remaining on top of the hedge. Jess climbed up and with one well gauged

Clearing the midden in the yard on a Devon farm, prior to spreading the muck on the land. This was one of the most backbreaking tasks in farming.

thrust, he split the tree trunk near to its base but only partially severing it, really splitting it so that it could be laid horizontally along the hedge leaning away from the split. The crooks, which we had cut, were then used to peg the tree down in the correct position ensuring that future off-shoots would grow upright. We continued in this fashion until all the selected trees were evenly laid and pegged. I left Jess to complete this task as I had to carry out my evening duties.

All that remained now was for the ditch to be dug out, cleared and the debris heaped up onto the hedgerow.

Laying a hedge in the correct manner was considered a work of art and I understand it is dying out as motorised hedge trimmers are taking over but a newly laid hedge looked wonderful particularly when the new growth sprouted.

MUCK SPREADING
The size of the dung heap or midden was now getting beyond a joke and I was aware that the appropriate time of year was upon us for its removal. I chivvied Mr Edwards about this 'thorn in my side' and he eventually succumbed and hired Art with his tractor and large trailer to come over so that we could dump this mountain of manure out in the fields. Mr Edwards and I climbed on top of the heap and loaded the dung into the trailer. It was then driven out to Pitfield where it was dumped in small heaps at regular intervals. This was repeated time and time again until every smelly forkful

was cleared from the farmyard. When we were roughly halfway through I happened to dig deep into the heap with my fork and as I raised it, the sight before me caused me to yell out. Underneath me, by my feet was a writhing mass of snakes. I just couldn't believe my eyes, Mr Edwards told me to get off the heap quickly and he and Art proceeded to kill every last one of these serpents. Yes they were poisonous snakes – zig zag marked adders, which had obviously hibernated within the midden where it was very warm.

I had my work cut out for the foreseeable future. All those mini dung heaps out in Pitfield had to be spread over the surface area of the field evenly. It was a stinky job and I would spend ages when the days work was done washing and deodorising myself conscious of the smell which seemingly clung, not only to my clothes, but to my skin.

Eventually the muck spreading was complete and a few heavy showers soon washed it into the ground. Best of all, the courtyard was unrecognisable. I gave it a good sluice and clean and it appeared to be twice its previous size.

It was around this time that one of our sheep got Scrapie, a brain affection. I felt so helpless witnessing its condition deteriorate for there was nothing to be done except isolate it from the flock until it died.

WICKED BOB

Art had invited Mr Edwards to accompany him to a cattle sale. This was the boss's ideal day out so Art duly collected him in his car and off they went. Pansy and Frolic were exercising in the paddock but Bob was in her stable. The stables needed mucking out and good brush up as the horses had been kept in during the severe weather. I placed the wheelbarrow by the stable door and cleared out the two vacant stalls replenishing the racks with fresh hay. Next I had to transfer Bob into one of the clean stalls in order to clear out the dung and wet straw from her cubicle. I spoke to her as I made to move up alongside her when all of a sudden she lashed out, hard and strong with her left hind leg, catching me on my leg above the knee. So vicious was the kick that it knocked me across the stable and I ended up elbows down in a large heap of horse manure. I really wondered what had hit me and was too shocked to move for quite some time. When I eventually attempted to get up my leg was extremely painful and I had to hop indoors. Mrs Edwards brought a bowl of warm water, cloth and soap and helped to wash me down while Gladys got help.

I was in my pyjamas when Nurse Heath arrived and examined my leg which by this time was red and swollen and I was relieved when she proclaimed that there was nothing fractured, just severe bruising. She ordered me to rest and I went up to bed for the remainder of the day. It was dark when the master returned and when told of my mishap, he asked his wife to get me up. Then he insisted that I accompany him to the stable and harness up Bob.

How sadistic was that!?!

"How can you expect me to do that?" I yelled at him

"See yer, maid, if thees don't do it now, thees'll never have nerve to work a hors again."

I took some convincing and I was shaking as I hobbled down to the stable alongside Mr Edwards who carried a storm lantern.

With false bravado I spoke firmly to Bob and although inwardly I felt very nervous, I threw the saddle over her back and continued until she was fully harnessed.

"Good girl, I know what that felt like," he said and I remembered that his leg had been badly broken from the kick of a horse. I nuzzled into Bob's soft mouth and forgave her. The family did the milking without me and the boss attended to Frolic, Pansy and Bob allowing me to go back to bed.

Gradually the swelling subsided leaving a huge horseshoe shaped bruise on my thigh – red, purple and yellow it turned and eventually disappeared. Nurse Heath assured me that I had been extremely fortunate. The blow had caught the fleshy part of my thigh but had it landed a little lower, my knee would have been smashed. My friends teased me mercilessly.

"Wounded in action" and "You'll be up for the VC now" were their jokey remarks.

A year later Mr Edwards led Bob by her rope halter out tot he top of Long Mead in order to release her. As he slipped the rope halter off over her head, Bob whipped around swiftly and, supported by her fore legs, she kicked out with both hind legs simultaneously just missing the boss by a hair's breadth. The following day a lorry belonging to Jotcham Bros., slaughters, from Langport whisked Bob away for ever.

* * *

On one particular weekend Alan had been unable to get leave and so on the Sunday afternoon I decided to pick some of my favourite violets, Mrs Edwards knew they were my favourite flowers and she told me she had seen quite a few of them on the hedge of Bob Shute's lane.

I was quietly picking my flowers when in the distance I heard the clip clopping of horses hoofs and as I turned I saw a pony and trap approaching. A man held the reins and seated behind him was a little old lady. As they approached me, the driver slowed down the pony to a walk and I backed as far into the side of the road as I could. Facing them I bade the lady "Good afternoon" then continued to collect my violets as the pony trotted on again. I thought no more about the incident until later that week when Mr Edwards informed me that the estate manager had sent him a message.

"Thee's done it now Mick," he said with a grin.

"What's that then?" I asked him, trying to work out what drastic thing I had perpetrated.

Seemingly the Lady in the pony trap whom I had encountered the previous Sunday had been (quite unknown to me) The Dowager, Lady Sidmouth, mother of his Lordship. Apparently my misdemeanour had been that although her groom had slowed down when approaching me, I had failed to curtsy.

Nobody had ever enlightened me regarding this custom but, on meeting Lord or Lady Sidmouth or the Dowager, it was considered respectful and mannerly to either bow to his Lordship or curtsy to his Ladies. Frankly I didn't wish to know.

I was and to this day still am in favour of respect and consideration but the days of subservience were long since gone. I never bowed or curtsied to anyone even though the other parishioners and tenants of His Lordship did.

ELECTIONS RESUMED

Now that the war was over parliamentary elections were resumed. For the duration of the war The Cabinet had consisted of MPs from all political persuasions. Mr Peart, a Labour MP, had been the Minister of Agriculture and the general consensus was that he had done an excellent job, sympathetic to the farmer's needs and generous in the granting of farm subsidies.

When the subject of politics arose and the impending elections discussed, I would tease Mr Edwards, insinuating that, as Mr Peart had served him so well, he would likely be giving Labour his vote.

"Doan 'ee let anyone 'ere ye zay that, maid, His Lordship wouldn't like it at all," he retorted. I was amazed that in some way he was still mentally persuaded by his 'Lord and Master' despite free and secret elections.

Labour were victorious despite the popularity of Mr Winston Churchill as a wartime leader.

MOTHER'S VISIT

It had been arranged for my mother to stay with me in the late Spring before haymaking was due to commence and although I looked forward to her visit I was deeply concerned. How would she cope with the lack of comfort and the living conditions?

When she first experienced my new lifestyle the answer was, "not very well". She liked the family but could in no way comprehend how I could be so contented with my lot, especially when during the night she would try to kill the mice running about my room by trying to wallop them with my Land Army brogue.

By now I never even took notice of the lack of amenities – it was the kindness and love of the people that meant so much to me. Whenever it was possible she would accompany me around the farm standing on one side whilst I got on with whatever task I had to do. She strolled out with me when I turned the cows out each evening fascinated when certain animals came over to me and tried to lick the pocket of my dungarees knowing that I always carried a few dairy nuts therein. (Mr Edwards told her that it was no longer a farm but a circus).

The final straw came when I was milking in a two-stalled byre. It was roomier than the long cow stalls and I was sitting under one cow when the other one turned with its rear end against me, lifted its tail and "plopped" directly over my head. Mother was aghast as she watched from the doorway but, taking it all in my stride, I just got up, strode over to the water trough and ducked the whole of my head beneath the water. The muck soon rinsed off so I just gave my head a good shake (my hair was short) and resumed milking my cows.

After that incident mum begged me to give it all up and return home to 'civilisation' with her. "It's criminal to expect a young woman to suffer such indignities," was her shocked opinion. The time passed by quickly and I don't think she was sorry when time came for her departure.

COUNTRY HUMOUR

Here are some anecdotes of occurrences around this time.

The aforementioned Bert whose farm bordered the A30 road did not own a bull. Therefore when any of his cows were ready for servicing he would drive them all the way down to Kitts Farm paying Mr Edwards a fee for the use of Ferdinand. On one such occasion we were all seated around the table taking our tea when there was a knock on the backhouse door.

"See to it, Mick," the boss requested of me.

When I opened the door Bert stood there, cow stick in hand and cattle dog to heel. He informed me that he had brought one of cows for servicing and that it was in the courtyard. In I went and passed on his message.

"I'm having me tea, he knows where the bull is. Ask him if he can managed hizzel." Out I trotted once more repeating the boss's message to Bert. He immediately poked his head around the door and shouted.

"Frank! Why the ell do ee think I've driven the bloody cow all this way if ah could a managed mizzel."

With hindsight I can now see the humour in his outburst but at that time I could just feel the colour rising up my neck and face culminating in a deep red blush. I was completely taken aback.

But that was dear old Bert! No offence meant and therefore none taken, just his simple, dry country humour.

The next amusing incident I recall could have been tragic.

The field where I had put the cows when I turned them out one evening had little grazing left and therefore I was asked to throw some mangolds from the cave situated in an adjacent field over the hedgerow to where the cows were grazing and thus supplement their diet. I went about my task hurling mangold after mangold over the hedge when I suddenly heard shouting and hollering coming from the other side. Nervously I peered over the hedge to find Mr Edwards seemingly quite stunned rubbing his head. He had been doing his evening patrol with his gun and his dog and had unwittingly strolled under a hail of mangolds! A mangold is a large, heavy, solid root and could have done untold damage. Although I worriedly apologised profusely he admitted that he should have been aware as he had given the order.

* * *

Through all the years of our association I only recall one altercation. This particular day I noticed that one of the cows had a nasty scratch from base to tip of one of her teats. Once I had tied up all the cows I went indoors for some Dettol and clean rag and proceeded to bath the teat with this antiseptic solution. Naturally the cow was restless whilst the operation was being carried out. Now Mr Edwards was wont to go from one cow to the next when milking until he felt the bucket was full enough to warrant a journey up to the churn for sieving. On this occasion I noticed that he was about to sit under the cow which had the painful scratch and that he had a considerable amount of milk in his bucket from the previous cow. "Mr Edwards" I called, "Don't you think you should try milking her with an empty pail?" She's damaged one teat and is restless."

"Her'll be alright," he rejoined and proceeded to milk.

It wasn't too long before I heard heated ejaculations and expletives followed by thuds. Jumping up from the cow I was milking I hurried to the stall to find him beating the offending cow with his three-legged milking stool whilst his pail laid horizontally on the cobbles which were covered with the spewed out milk.

I was completely incensed at his actions particularly as he had been advised of the situation, I quickly placed myself between him and the cow and fists at the ready I warned (and I am not in the habit of swearing), "Now, you bugger if you want to vent your temper try it on me and see what you get."

There was a ghastly silence then he put his tool down and burst out laughing. He laughed and laughed although he later admitted that I had scared him half to death. He admitted he had been way out of line and told everyone the story ending with "Nobody will be hurting my stock, that's for sure."

This incident was quite out of character for him as I believe he was the most gentle, considerate man I have ever met. He had deep religious beliefs and I never heard him swear in the true sense of the word. I guess it was just one occasion when he lost it entirely.

* * *

Finally their springs to mind the time when it was decided to reseed the field above the hayshed orchard. It all ended well otherwise it could have been tragic.

The field had been ploughed and worked down in preparation for sowing the grass seed. Art came over towing the drill behind his tractor. Mr Edwards positioned himself on the platform at the rear of the drill in order to control the levers for the dispersal of the seed and it was my job to stand by the hedge where stood a large sackful of seed. When the boss signalled I was to run over to him with two buckets of seed and refill the seed box.

At the outset all went according to plan as the tractor driven by Art traversed up and down the field and Mr Edwards ensured that the seed was correctly and evenly distributed over the earth. Then I heard a familiar yell and looking up from my task of filling the supply buckets I saw that the bar connecting drill to tractor had worked loose tipping the drill forward, upending it. Mr Edwards was straddled over the top of the drill with his head just a few inches from the ground and his legs waving about in the air. Art, completely unawares, was calmly driving on up the field. I rushed over and helped the boss become earthbound (the right way up) at the same time shouting loudly and eventually attracting Art's attention.

I was splitting my sides with laughter at the sight of the boss upside down – my wicked sense of humour – but admittedly it shook him up. He wasn't injured, apart form his vanity, so 'all's well that ends well'.

On an earlier occasion I had been fascinated whilst watching Jess Hunt sowing a field of corn using the old fashioned method of a fiddle. The method we had used to reseed our field that day was at that time considered up to date.

Proposal

Alan considered that his demobilisation from the Royal Navy was imminent. He was being given longer periods of leave enabling us to spend more time together. Two problems arose in our relationship, which affected me and caused me to take a step back and think deeply about the future. That I was deeply in love with him, I had no doubt but, being long term in the Royal Navy, he drank a lot of rum and on many occasions he was drunk – too many occasions in my estimation. My father had been a heavy drinker, which resulted in years of misery for my mother and our family in general and finally resulted in the breakdown of his marriage. I had witnessed at first hand what this love of the bottle could do, changing a funny, affectionate loving man into a monster and so it was a flaw which I had to consider very seriously. It saddened me tremendously.

The second problem was less serious yet there was little I could do to solve it. For some unfathomable reason Alan's mother refused to be introduced to me, she was adamant that I was not a suitable girlfriend for her son despite the fact that our paths had not so far crossed. On meeting, his father always acknowledged me, as did the rest of his family. I became concerned when Alan did not put in an appearance one evening as we had arranged and when he failed to show up the following evening I became quite worried.

I dithered over my decision but finally plucked up the courage and walked over to Little Common, the cottage where the Shire family lived. I knocked on the door but there was no response so I knocked harder. It was quite some time before Alan's father appeared and he did not invite me in when I enquired after his son, but brusquely said, "He's bad and they've taken him into hospital." With that he shut the door. Which hospital I wondered?

I half walked, half ran all the way back to Kitts Farm with tears streaming down my cheeks and as usual Mrs Edwards tried to comfort and console me assuring me I was too good for that family adding the old cliché "there's more fish in the sea". The truth was, it was Alan I wanted.

The evening wore on and when we were preparing to go to bed there came a hard knock on the door. As it was late Mr Edwards insisted on answering it and returned to tell me that Alan's brother, Frank, wished to speak to me. I knew that Frank had recently returned from service in the

Left: *Alan in 1946.* Above: *Maud (the author) and Alan on Honeymoon in Blackpool, 1946.*

Far East, Burma I believe, and he had recently been demobbed from the RAF but I had not realised that he was at his parent's home because he had recently married. He introduced himself to me and briefly explained that Alan had taken ill quite suddenly and had been admitted into Whipton Isolation Hospital in Exeter. Apparently he had succumbed to a strain of diphtheria, was perilously ill and needed to be isolated.

Frank was very kind and understanding. He even explained that, at that moment in time, he was having similar problems in as much as his mother had not approved of his marriage or his wife who was pregnant. "We're just hoping she'll see sense," he said. Although I was extremely worried for Alan I could at least go to him now – comfort and support him.

When I finally arrived at the hospital I was met at the door to his ward by the Sister who kindly explained that Alan had been very close to death's door but had survived the crisis and although still extremely ill, he had a good chance of pulling through. I asked if I could see him so she directed me to a certain window and told me to wait there. I was not allowed in the ward for obvious reasons.

As I peered through the window a nurse kindly turned his bed around so that I could face him but he looked dreadfully sick. He did manage a weak smile when I mouthed the words, "I love you, hang in there". It was such a brief visit but it somehow put my mind at rest.

I visited him on every possible occasion over the following weeks and each time he appeared to be a little bit stronger. For the length of his sojourn at Whipton I was not allowed inside but finally that wicked wink was back. I was balancing on a log beneath his window one day and he pre-

HMS Colombo *in Malta.*

tended to kiss me – our lips met but with the glass between – when right out of the blue he said, "Will you marry me?"

As the subject of marriage or commitment had never hitherto arisen I was unprepared for this proposal and it was quite some time before I managed the word "Yes".

The following week Alan's cousin, Renee, called at the farm and asked if I would collect his clothes and take them down to Whipton Hospital as Alan was to be discharged. Saturday dawned and I strolled over to Little Common. Tentatively I knocked on the door and his mother came out and handed me a large brown paper parcel neatly tied up with string.

I had hoped that the ice would be broken by our joint concern for Alan's well-being and that she would accept me but few words were spoken as I remained in the porch. And so Alan came home.

We decided to keep our betrothal secret until he could buy my ring but we were so very happy and so very much in love.

* * *

Just around the corner big decisions had to be made. After serving for almost five years in the Navy adjusting to civilian life was going to be difficult. He went into the Navy just a boy and came out a man; service life had therefore played a huge part in his life. For two years he had served on HMS *Colombo* escorting convoys in the Mediterranean Sea, supporting the invasions of Sicily and Italy, aiding the Yugoslavians and taking part in a mock invasion of Southern France. (The latter was to draw away German attention from Normandy where the D Day landings took place). He had been wounded in both legs and had witnessed the most horrendous scenes, which traumatised him for most of his life.

We would both need employment and so many others were in an identical situation so we knew work would be difficult to find. Where were we to live? All these problems had to be discussed and solved but for the immediate future we were just determined to be together no matter what.

On 11th June 1946, my birthday, we became officially engaged. Jewellery was very scarce and we decided our money would be needed to set up a home of some sort so I diplomatically chose a neat ring – just one small diamond set in platinum and gold. Yet had it been the Koh-I-noor itself I could not have loved a ring more. I wore it on a chord around my neck whilst working but each evening it would be placed on the third finger of my left hand and gazed at with love and pride. Alan and I celebrated our engagement together early in July by going to Honiton Fair. Alan had purchased my ring at Shepherd's, the jewellers in Honiton (now Lunn Poly).

But we knew we had to come down to earth and make some really serious decisions. Later we made a brief visit to my home at Rishton where introductions were made and a date for our wedding was arranged in September. On our return we discussed our situation in earnest. I loved life in Devon enraptured by the beautiful scenery and I really wanted to remain in the south whereas Alan had travelled widely and was more ambitious. Eventually I realised that there was no lucrative employment in this area and agreed temporarily to move back up north. An added incentive was that my mother offered us the use of two rooms in her large house until we could acquire a house of our own.

Our immediate future had been decided.

* * *

Alan's love of rum was still causing me great concern and the situation finally came to a head when he got very, very inebriated one Saturday night and I had to support him all the way back to the farm. I knew that in no way could I tolerate a future facing such behaviour and I called off the engagement there and then, handed back the ring and heartbroken ran into the farmhouse.

I never knew how Alan managed to get back home – he was in such a state and a week passed by without word of him. He eventually turned up the following weekend and asked me to give him another chance and take back the ring. Realising I would be back to square one I was adamant that I could never share my life with a toper.

"Please Maud," he begged, "I promise that if you give me a second chance I'll never drink rum again – I'll not get drunk."

I guess I was naïve but he did seem so positive.

"Promises, promises!" I said sardonically, "Okay but the first time you do get drunk now will be the last as far as I am concerned," was my ultimatum.

I allowed him to replace his ring on my finger and we resumed our relationship. At this point, I must add that he cut out his rum drinking completely – he had an occasional glass of beer but he kept his word to me. Excessive drinking was never a cause for worry during the years of our union.

Life returned to normal and, of course, the following weeks were once again exceedingly busy workwise, with the repeat of haymaking, harvesting, etc. It was also quite a sad time for me because Whiteface, my Hereford cow, had complications whilst calving. Despite the vet's best efforts my poor Whiteface lost her life as did her calf.

APPLEDORE

I had worked continuously for several weeks forfeiting my half day off each week so that I could have a long weekend with Alan at Appledore – an arrangement agreed with the boss. Frankly I was feeling in need of a rest.

The sun was shining as I set out to catch the train, firstly to Exeter then on to Bideford. Alan was on duty and could not meet me and I travelled by taxi from Bideford to his billet at Appledore arriving in the late afternoon. His landlady and her family were exceptionally kind to me and brought out tea and cakes.

Alan eventually came in and was so very pleased to see me. He was keen to take me on a tour of this quaint and beautiful town. It had been arranged for me to stay with another family member further away from the River front for my three day visit. We spent a wonderfully restful weekend together. Alan introduced me to his peers and gave me a conducted tour of fascinating Bideford and the delightful town of Appledore. He pointed out the various Royal Naval ships at anchor and the intriguing little alleyways of the town. The buildings were mainly quaint fishermen's cottages and the inns and were unbelievably 'olde worlde'.

The following day we strolled over to Westward Ho! and basked in the warm sunshine on its endless sandy beach where we witnessed the landing of several dukws (amphibious landing craft). I even managed to swim in the open air swimming pool.

Eventually after a lovely meal, we leisurely ambled back to Appledore; arms entwined, enthralled by the beautiful sunset reflected on the water. Alan was on duty early the following day and I had to catch the train back but the memory of that precious break will remain with me always. I'm sure the rest was badly needed because I returned to work full of new found enthusiasm and vigour.

Helping with the haymaking at Kitts Farm in later years. From left to right: Towser (the cattle dog), Galdys, Sport (gun dog), Margaret, Harry Edwards, Frank Edwards and Alan.

FAREWELL TO DEVON

Mr and Mrs Edwards were quite perturbed at the prospect of my departure but they were happy for me too. Gladys was near to school leaving age and would be able to step into my shoes, which soothed my conscience to a great extent.

Our association had forged very strong links in the chain of friendship, which would last a lifetime. In later years Mr Edwards was the godfather to our first born, Margaret, and in return Margaret was a bridesmaid when Gladys married. They nursed, supported and cared for me during a very difficult pregnancy.

We had to return to Rishton for many practical reasons but I never, ever settled there again and it was not long after we were married that we returned to my beloved West Country. Alan and I had a beautiful wedding. We were married on 7th September at the Parish Church in Rishton.

As I end these memoirs the year is 2005 and in twelve months' time, God willing, we will celebrate our diamond wedding – sixty years together. There have been many ups and downs over these years but we are still in love.

Nineteen forty six saw the ending of my single life as a Land Girl but it was also the beginning of another era, another story, another saga.

Photographs taken at the reunion of the Women's Land Army at Totnes, Devon, on 2nd April 2005.

ADDENDUM

I am now, of course, Maud Shire. Micky Mitchell was the same person in a different time warp. I still live in my beloved West Country, at Honiton where hopefully I will spend the remainder of my days.

Alan and I had four beautiful daughters, Margaret, Rosemary, Elaine and Vanessa and our youngest child is a son, Alan. We currently have thirteen grandchildren, twelve great-grandchildren and many step-grandchildren – all of whom we love dearly.

Sadly Alan has suffered from multiple sclerosis for many years and now needs twenty-four hour care in a Royal British Legion Nursing Home at nearby Taunton.